Why
Still Like This Only

To
Dear Veerji &
Teela Bahenji
with warm regards
& Thank you for all the help

25/10/10

Dr. Jaideep Singh Chadha, MD

DIAMOND BOOKS

ISBN : 978-81-288-2946-8

© Author

Published by
Diamond Pocket Books Pvt. Ltd.
X-30, Okhla Industrial Area, Phase-II
New Delhi-110020
Phone : 011-41611861, 40712100
Fax : 011-41611866
E-mail : sales@dpb.in
Website : www.dpb.in

Edition : 2010

Printed by
Adarsh Printers, Delhi-110032

Why are We Still Like This Only
Dr. Jaideep Singh Chadha, MD

Dedication

This book is dedicated to

Dr. Manmohan Singh
the Prime Minister of India

Our freedom fighters

All ranks of the armed forces

*Mr. Khushwant Singh
for being there, so that
I can hero-worship him*

and

to my lovely grand daughter
MEHAR
*a picture of innocence
honesty and trust*

"Pity the nation that is full of beliefs and devoid of religion.

Pity the nation that acclaims the bully as hero and that deems the glittering conqueror when it's bountiful.

Pity the nation that raises not it's voice save when it walks in a funeral, boasts not except among its ruins and will rebel, not save, when its neck is laid between the sword and the block.

Pity the nation whose statesman is a fox, whose philosopher is a juggler and whose art is the art of patching and mimicking.

Pity the nation that welcomes its new ruler with trumpeting and farewells him with hootings, only to welcome another with trumpetings again.

Pity the nation divided into fragments, each fragment deeming itself a nation."

– *Kahlil Gibran*
"The Garden of the Prophet"

Acknowledgements

If Indians had been as honest as the British, as sophisticated as the French, as disciplined and hardworking as the Germans, as proud of their heritage, culture and traditions as the Japanese and the Chinese, as passionate about freedom as the Israelis, then this book would never have seen the light of day. Unfortunately, we are none of these. Indians are indeed masters in the art of trading and making money, especialy under the table.

My eernal gratitude to my parents, Late Sardar Iqbal Singh Chadha, my father, who was the most honest person I have ever known and Mrs Harbhajan Kaur, my mother, who inculcated in us the basics of honesty.

I am thankful to my wife, Gurminder Kaur, for being there always.

I am gateful to Sardar Preminder Singh Sandhawalia, Lord of Rdwick, author and golfer, for his patience and his comments on the book. Can one be uplifted more than when a person like Mr Sandhawalia asks, "If you don't need it, can I keep this copy. I would like the whole of my family to read it!"

How can I forget my friend SJS Panwar. No book of mine can go into the publishers' den without first being scrutinized by him. Thanks, Sam!

Immense gratitude to Major Rajinder Singh Bhatti, my daughter Guneet Kaur Bhatti, my son Aman Deep and my daughter-in-law, Chandni, for their inputs and advice. I also thank my friend, Amar Grewal, because he has been associated with this book right from the first draft. Professor Meera Malik and my friend Mrs. Chanda Jain also deserve special encomium for their encouragement and appreciation of whatever I do.

I am thankful to Mr Narender Verma of Diamond Publications and his team for the work put in by them.

And then there is Ajit Singh Walia.

— **Dr. Jaideep Singh Chadha**, *MD*

Author's Note

Every country has a story revolving around its people and events that affected it. This story becomes its' history when it covers a large time frame. Bharat has a long history. But somebody changed the name of our country from Bharat to India and over the years, Bharat, Hindustan and India have been used whimsically. There are countries like France which give India funny names like Indie. When they can keep calling their own country France, why should they change ours to Indie? It is because, we let them. That is why! The natives of countries like the USA and UK start calling Indians living in their countries by non-Indian pet names like Jimmy, Tom or James and so many others. Their excuse is that the pronunciation of Indian names is difficult. Have they ever seriously tried? They can pronounce a tongue-twisting Russian or Polish name alright but when they come to an Indian name, they refuse to do so. Schwartzneiger is a really difficult name to pronounce. No one thought of changing his name to Warty or Nigger. So, why change Jaswant Singh or Pritam Pillai to Jimmy or Tammy? The Indians are too eager to 'integrate' into that society, so instead of sticking to their own names, they are proud to become Betty, Tim or James. Even a Chinese sticks to his own name. Why do we let people play with something as personal as our names? Don't our names represent our identity? Or, do we end up saying, "Oh! What is there in a name?"

I am not really bothered about these NRIs letting white people change their names but I definitely do not want the name of my country changed. **It is confusing for the young, nay everyone, because we don't know what the name of our country really is. Is it Bharat, Hindustan, India or Indie?** Can we settle this first? Our 'glorious' freedom of 63 years can come later. This is just an example. Why do we let the world play around with us? Why have we been like this? **Why are we still like this only?**

It would be so easy to write about the positive stuff Indians are made of. I could write about the "half-full glass" and "the doughnut and not the hole!" I could write poems about how rich the Indians are, how honorable and un-corruptible we are. I could also write about our culture, how we treat each other with respect and love and live like brothers; our traditions, where we treat our elderly women as our mothers and the young ones as our sisters; the fantastic food that we get here, the unsurpassed beauty of our cities and villages. I could go on to tell you about our materialistic progress and achievements in the world of science. I could also tell you about our heroic exploits in the world of sport.

But all this would just be a hollow lie. There has to be someone to show you the true picture. Moreover, you have to be ready to see the truth as it is and not as you would deem it to be. Only then would things begin to change.

This book is not an autobiography. The little things that I have told you about myself are only to bring you into the proper prospective in relation to the time period that I describe. This book has been inspired by pseudosophisticated Indians who have the temerity to laugh it off when someone furnishes facts and figures to prove that Indians are a highly corrupt people or some of our politicians deserve capital punishment for their deeds or when someone tells you that we not only adulterate all our edible and non edible products, but also our thoughts. They go on to discuss the current trends over a cup of coffee or a drink in the evening and think that their duty towards the country is over. Ladies and gentlemen, these issues should not to be laughed away, for matters have reached such pitiable states only because we have trivialized them for too long.

–Dr. Jaideep Singh Chadha, MD

"Power will go to the hands of rascals and rogues and freebooters. All Indian leaders will be of low caliber and men of straw. They will have sweet tongues and silly hearts. They will fight among themselves for power. India will be lost in political squabbles. A day would come when air and water would taxed in India."

– Sir Winston Churchill

We are incredible people! We proved that he was right.

Preface

We Indians believe that we are the best in the world. That belief might well be true. *In the words of John Locke, the famous philosopher, "There is no truth. Truth is what one wants to believe."* Over the years, I have tried to ascertain the veracity of this statement. I find Locke's statement completely true. There is, in fact, no truth. An event which occurred a few days, months or years ago can be interpreted in any way one wants to and can be propagated in any way it suits the propagator. But for the masses it will be always be the truth, if, they want to believe it as the truth.

I have always believed that there is no country better or more beautiful than India. One could argue that I have not yet seen the entire world. But just consider these facets of India. Our society is a fabric made flom of multi-lingual and multicultured threads. India has, since times immemorial, been the fountainhead of spirituality. India believed in the lofty ideals of dignity and respect of the individual in society.

In the epic Ramayana, there is the mention of Udhan Khatolas and atomic weapons; if they were the product of a writer's imagination, we have to respect the man for imagining all that years much before the West invented the motor car!

We had divine souls like Guru Nanak, Gautama Buddha, Swami Vivekananda, Ananda Mayi Ma, Aurobindo and a host of other great spiritualists. The list is so long that a whole book could be written about the great people who inhabited India in the Dark Ages. I wonder, though, if those were the Dark Ages or if we are actually living in a dark age now?

We have had our warriors but these warriors could not sacrifice their ego to knit India into a strong and powerful nation. India was one of the richest countries of the world, till we got repeatedly plundered by barbarians, who took advantage of our being non martial to a large degree and patriotic in fits and starts!

Even as my love for my motherhood made me smug, things were changing at a surprising speed and the transformation shook me out of the complacence. The spiritual aspect of India had disappeared even before my generation made its appearance. Our ancestors had fallen to the Mughuls and then, the British, who managed to rule over us for more than 200 years. In doing so, they got the support from the very people they had vanquished. Did they really conquer India, or was it that the Indians surrendered their freedom easily, which, for most people of the world, really, is their lifepline, self respect and their right to self governance? Luckily, my generation came along when the British had left.

When the British decided to effect their coup de grace for the subcontinent, what they left as a legacy was a **Bharat** divided into India and Pakistan. Thanks to the colonialist's "divide and rule" policy and the resultant discord and bitterness created between generally peaceful, secular and tolerant people, untold misery was heaped on millions of the two nations. Who is responsible for the carnage? Was it the British? Or was it the peoples of the two countries? Was it the handiwork of a handful of politicians, or can we call religion as a culprit?

Who will answer these questions?

India had to rebuild itself in the backdrop of shattered confidences. The shackles of foreign domination still had their impact. Leaders of that time had very little knowledge of how to run a country as big as India which was reeling under the wounds and sores of partition and relief camps. Millions of people had lost their near and dear ones. Indians had remained dormant for so long under the British that they had developed the habit of always waiting for their British masters to tell them what to do and how. Eventually, Bharat attained her independence on 15th August, 1947. At the stroke of midnight, Pandit Jawahar Lal Nehru had his moment of glory when, as the first Prime Minister of free India, he gave his speech of the *"tryst with destiny"* which still reverberates in the annals of Bharats' history. Once the initial euphoria was over, we should have set about erasing the humiliating memory of the 200 years that had scarred our past forever. We should have reverted to Bharat instead of being called India. But, independence day continues to be celebrated in the hope that it will be always serve as a reminder for future generations that we should never let that happen again. So, we ended up saying that we have now existed for 60 years! As if Bharat did not exist before that. The younger generation gives two hoots for what happened so many years ago. For them, Independence Day is just a holiday but we still keep on celebrating it.

Nevertheless, Indians do love their country and we are a patriotic lot. We have fought wars with Pakistan and been victorious every time. In the war with China where India took a beating because we were under-prepared for a war, too lax and did not realize how much progress China had made and how strong it had become. Meanwhile, Bollywood, made movies showing our brave warriors fighting a superior enemy and sacrificing their lives so that their country-men would never have to re-live the ignominy of slavery again. They upped the pride quotient of Indians on the celluloid canvass.

Running a country should be easy if one understands the principles of division of labor. One group runs the internal aspect of the country. Another looks after our image, trade and our financial security in the international scenario. Still another group looks after the protection of our citizens; they are armed forces. There is a very important group which constitutes the country and that is the citizenry of the country. On paper, this group looks very innocuous. In India, they would be the religious fanatics, political goons and those interested in only making money for themselves. They indude the corporate sector, individual businessman and crooks and criminals which give us our corrupt element. If this group of the corrupt elements becomes too powerful and too successful, it starts running the country's finance, foreign affairs and politics. It is then that a country is in for serious trouble; and we are in trouble mind!

Moving on to the sports arena, India discovered a game of hockey. We were good at playing it. In fact, we were very good. Major Dhyan Chand was an acknowledged wizard. We were the champion nation in hockey. But the fall has been stupendous. Today, we stand nowhere in international hockey. First, it was the men's team which failed to qualify for the Olympics. Then, the women's team failed too. In athletics, India's recognition has been limited to two stars, Milka Singh, and P.T. Usha. Years later, Abhinav Bindra won the gold medal in shooting in the Beijing Olympics, making it India's debut individual gold medal in the history of Olympics. This was followed by two medals in boxing and wrestling, Vijendra Kumar and Sushil Kumar being the respective winners. They have undoubtedly brought great glory to India.

Abhinav Bindra was hardly thought to be the one to bring any medal for India, for all eyes were on Major Rathod expecting a repeat performance. I personally had even forgotten which Abhinav's patent event was. *When the gold medal arrived, the country was in a frenzy. Poets penned poems in his praise. Some companies signed him as their brand ambassador. And the public will do what it knows best and will forget him before the next Olympic games, hoping that he loses so that they can eulogize a new hero!*

In cricket, we have had our moments of glory and some even of shame. We have the greatest living batsmen in Sunil Gavaskar and Sachin Tendulkar. Professional wrestling, as a sports event has given us our new god, Khalli. In many fields of intellect, our children are frontrunners. Arjun Atwal has won a US PGA event in geef since is happen to be the first US tour victory by an Indian. We are ecstatic. Jeev Milkha Singh, the son of the legendary Milkha Singh, and Gagandeep Singh Bhullar are making good strides in golf. We have young Rahul Bakshi, who won the Faldo International Series Junior Golf in Brazil in 2008 and then, went on to become the youngest winner of the National Amateur golf championship the same year. Further, twelve-year-old Zoravar Singh Thiara, of Chandigarh, is ranked 8th in Asia in the equesprian sport. He is preparing for the 2014 Junior Olympics in Germany. Let us hope for the best. We have world champions in boxing (Vijendra Singh), billiards and chess too. Mary Kom, who is a champion in world boxing (women) and has won titles five times, has done wonders. She is also a mother. *But, they are like fresh snowflakes which melt away even before we have had a chance to savor them. We need them to come up in droves, like a swarm of locusts. They must make the world sit up and take notice. That is what we need and not just sporadic mushroomial brilliance.*

Yet another malady that is noticeable is the breakdown of the joint family and the loss of family values. Interpersonal relationships within the family and society are hardly given any credence. Materialism is a cancer which is affecting the world over but the younger generation is the one which has been hit the hardest. Money *is* the yardstick of success.

This book is an attempt to help wake up my compatriots out of their slumber. We have to rise above petty personal agendas if India is to become great again. Really speaking, we cease to exist if India perishes!

My special friend is SaMule, who I met in Kanpur. We were watching the same "fight-to-the-death" scenario. Two hoodlums were slugging it out and then, one of them decided to show the other guy's entrails by slitting open his tummy with a huge knife. I became sick and vomited. But SaMule had been very clinical about the whole thing. He just uttered "what a waste, what a waste." After bidding me farewell, he disappeared. I met him again in Chandigarh and we became great friends. I found him extremely intelligent and so full of humor that I decided to take him along with me to seek his opinion on complicated subjects affecting the Indian paradoxes.

–Jaideep Singh Chadha
jaichadha2007@gmail.com

Contents

1

India: A Country with Contrasts

I have heard a particular Hindi song for so many years now and it has stayed with me since the day I first heard it. It is a song about India. Here is a verse

Jahan dal dal par soney ki chidiya
karti hain basera
Vo Bharat Desh hai nera
Jai Bharti, Jai Bharti, Jai Bharti!

Praising Bharat, and hailing victory to her, the verse talks of how the country is so rich and blessed with plenitude that it could be compared to a tree with sparrows made of pure gold.

This song, which you may also sung I, was the fantasy of a great poet. Poets have the ability and the talent to shake nations and move the masses with their words. I heard it for the first time on the popular program of Radio Ceylon, called 'Binaca Geet Mala!' It was compeered by the well known Amin Sayani. This song is now heard mostly around Republic days and Independence Days, when the patriotic sentiment is high! I salute the poet. I have only heard stories of the glory of what India was in the distant past. I am however a witness to the deterioration of India in certain areas as also the progress in others. I am a part of whatever is happening to India and in India. Is India disintegrating? Well, if the poet who wrote this wonderful song, well alive today, he would definitely have rephrased it.

The former President of the United States of America, Mr. George W. Bush Jr, was in the news for the wrong reason, as always. He threw a few pearls of wisdom of his own creation. He opined that the food shortage in the world and the rising oil prices were because of Indians because Indians ate too much. Earlier, Indians could not afford two- and four-wheelers. Now, everyone in India does. That is how the oil shortage began. Like many people in the country, I too took great umbrage to that statement. I am a human and to get angry with others is my birthright. I told SaMule about it .

"Obviously, Mr. President hasn't heard of the song penned by the great poet or of the past glory of India. It isn't his fault. Basically, the world is full of ignoramuses who live in their small limited worlds. For average Americans, their world is only up to as the boundaries of their individual states or cities. For them, to know about their own country is a very big job. So, knowing about a country like India is next to impossible. When he took over as President of the USA, he did not even know who the Prime Minister of India was! He probably had no need to know. He was surrounded by enough people who would give him that information if and when he needed it. After many years of being in office, someone had informed him that Indians were now eating two meals a day! And that their middle class has become affluent enough to buy vehicles and they are gobbling up the world's food and oil. As if we don't produce our own food and do not have our own oil! The fact still remains that 250 million of our countrymen do not get anything to eat at night and most of them are women and children. **I just hope his successor does not consider India a "WMC"– weapon of mass consumption and go after us as Bush went after Iraq for its oil, hiding behind the "WMD" or the "weapons of mass destruction theory,"** he said, exuding knowledge and wisdom.

I agreed. India has been looked upon as a country where poverty rules, snake charmers roam the streets, people can commute only on foot and many people subsist on one meal a day. The sight of huge Americans who can easily gobble large amounts of food and waste equal, nay greater, amounts, probably falls on the international retinal blind spot. The plastic and paper that they use and discard wantonly is shameful.

India has been changing over the years. It has made great strides in modern science. Today, we excel in so many areas. Yet, India has not established itself as a great power to reckon with. Why?

❑

2

1954-1965

My father worked in the ordnance wing of the Indian Army. Life in the forces in those days differed from civilian jobs because they were transferred after every three years. So, we had a chance to visit places all over the country. We went down south, to Chennai, to Jabalpur in Central India, to Kanpur, in the state of Uttar Pradesh and finally, to Pune in Maharashtra.

I was too young while we were in Chennai. In the Blue Blocks of Jabalpur Cantonment, we enjoyed growing up in a group of like-minded army officers' children. It was great fun to be able to roam uninhibitedly in the jungles of the area and have picnics on the water reservoir on the hill. This reservoir supplied water to the entire area where we lived. It took us an hour to climb up the hill and half of that time to come down. We used to collect flowers of Sambal trees to make colored water for Holi. The whole day was spent playing marbles and cricket. My brother and I were the local marble champions and we had jarfuls of the most colorful marbles and a huge collection of metallic ones which were basically ball bearings of different sizes made out of different metals. Those were actually their weight in gold for us. Colonel Hari Singh's Alsatian dog, George, would always be our fielder when we played cricket. No matter how hard we hit, it would jump and catch the ball in it's mouth.

According to our rules, the batsman used to be given out if George took the catch. Incidentally, dogs in India are always named George, Tommy or Harry. Indian names somehow don't sound good on them. The other Hari Singh was a major and he had a domesticated deer. It did not play cricket with us but it did lead the army parade. I don't remember what he was called but it responded to its' name. Major Hari Singh had to hand the deer over to the army authorities who, in turn, sent it to the zoo. Thus, we spent our days in the sleepy hamlet; and in the evenings, we had to be dragged back home by our parents. Home work and studies made up some part of the day but the memory of those moments is very hazy.

Those were the days when one saw children playing outdoors with no fear of being kidnapped. We had our own army club where my brothers and I learnt swimming — never mind the fact that I sank like a metal block when the sealed Dalda oil canister tied to my back got loose. It seemed to me as if I had swallowed the entire water of the pool! I still have a hazy memory of sinking into the pool very slowly and no matter what I tried, there was nothing I could do to prevent my sinking. My shouting made me swallow more water. I could see the canister bobbing on the surface and it seemed to distance itself from me as I sank. And then powerful arms lifted me out of the water. It was ny father who began pumping my chest and tummy. When I really came to, I was busy spurting water from my mouth like a whale. Interestingly, many years later, when I was in Illorin, Nigeria, my son who was 3 years old at the time was asked by an American lady who was the acting lifeguard for the evening, if he could swim.

"Yes!" he had said and had promptly jumped into the rubber pool. The lady had waited for him to come out and when he didn't, she jumped in and fished him out just I had been. He had no idea what being able to swim meant.

Back to my childhood, I was admitted into Christ Church School, an English medium school. My memories revolve around about how I spent most of my time in class, standing on my chair and getting beaten with foot ruler as punishment for one reason or the other. Mrs. Gupta, the class teacher, was very much against me. It was obvious that she had something against the Sikhs.

She would say, *"Sardarji, tumarey barah bajaa doongi!"* I was just six years old! I had no idea why she would say that again and again. When I asked my parents, no one remembered the basis of this statement. What infuriated my father was that Mrs. Gupta had to bring out her mean tenoeranebt against small children. So, he paid her a visit. He had a short temper and *what* he said to her and how it was said, made a difference. Instead, it was replaced with "stand up on your chair, you duffer!" I could never get this thing out of my mind really.

One day, my good friend, Mr. Latta, who produces films, came to the clinic. He has the full low-down on the infamous 12 o'clock jinx in regard to the Sikhs. Here is his narrative:

"When the Moghuls had taken over India under Ahmad Shah Abdali, Mir Manu was the governor of Punjab. Around that time, the Sikhs had formed a group which was named the Dal Khalsa. Masa Rangarh had taken over the Golden Temple and as a mark of contempt, he got the pond or sarovar filled up with mud. He got girls to dance in the gurudwara. The Sikhs would fill it up with water only to be filled with mud by Masa Rangarh again. Sukha Singh and Mehtab Singh were two Sikhs who had decided to kill Masa Rangarh. They entered the parikrama area where the sacred beri tree stands even today, posing as merchants. They called him to show what they had in their gunny bag. As Masa rangarh bent down, one of them chopped off Masa's head, which fell into the bag and the two ran away with it. They had to hide in the jungles for a long time after that.

Meanwhile, the Moghuls soldiers used to carry off Hindu women from villages as a sport. The Dal Khalsa brigade would attack the Mughuls at around mid-night when every one would be sleeping and rescue those women. It was the Moghuls who had coined the term *"sikhon key barah baj gayey."* They were afraid of the Sikhs. The Sikhs raided the enemy camps to rescue Hindu women." And today, the Sikhs are on the receiving end of a statement coined by the Moghuls! What an irony.

I am sure Mrs. Gupta, my teacher did not know anything about this historical fact but since it was passed on to many generations, she repeated it time and again. Over the years, I have been on the receiving end of such jibes. And I learned that all I had to do was be equally pungent and occasionally aggressive to make it stop, although not completely. *It came as a surprise in July 2010, when Bollywood actress, Priyanka Chopra, chosen as the host for a TV show, staring into the camera, says that she has finally got 13 people for the show, "aur ab inkay bajengey, barah!" I doubt if she even knows what she is talking about.*

While on the subject of teachers, let me tell you about the Hindi teacher we had in BNSD Inter College. We were in the ninth class. He was a sadist and at the slightest provocation, he would slap students with such a force that they would be lifted bodily by about 6 inches and crash into whatever was behind them. He would then catch them by the collar and proceed to slap them repeatedly. To the rest of us the sound of the slaps would reverberate in the room like thunder after a lightening strike. We would cower behind our desks. No one ever took any action against him. If the authorities did not, neither did we get together and beat him. I wonder in hindsight, why? The worst case scenario would have been getting kicked out of school. We would have shifted to some other institution. *However, we suffered him patiently. But, isn't that what we do even today? We go on suffering tyrants. When we are confronted with them, we continue to suffer them because of our fear of their power and their goons. That is how we sustain political tyrants.*

When my father was transferred to Kanpur the scenario changed very suddenly. We got to play and mix with civilian children. There was none of the closeness between families that we had in Jabalpur. We lived in the cantonment area which was separated from the congested colony by a railway line which passed just behind our house. So, every time a train went by, which was every half an hour or so, everything sort of rumbled in our house. We got over that pretty quickly since nothing toppled over and broke. There was a vacant piece of land adjacent to our house and we used that as a cricket ground. In the month of October or November, it would become a site for the Ram Lila celebrations. On the far side, there was a drain in which flowed filthy black stinking water. It probably passed through the colony. When a batsman hit a four, the tennis ball would land in the drain. The poor fellow fielding on the boundary would have to fish it out. All of us had to do it when our turn came. *If you had to play there, then the drain had to be accepted. That is how we learnt to accept things as they were.* The point is that none of us suffered from any skin disease or diarrhoea.

St Aloysius School, where we studied, was near by, just ahead of the Katehri Bagh. This was a huge park which was full of Jackfruit trees, laden with the enormously large jackfruit. Jackfruit is called 'katahal', hence the park's name, Katehri bagh. Next to it was the Defence Services Club which was a place for my badminton and swimming stints.

In many ways Kanpur is the city where I began to understand life as a twelve-years-old boy. Jabalpur was a neat, laid back city whereas Kanpur was a dirty, bustling industrial city, with people on the move all the time. It was the summer of 1957 that I arrived in this city, sitting in the window seat of the sleeper class compartment of the train that brought us from Jabalpur. As it trudged into the periphery of the railway yard of Kanpur central station., I found the rear walls of houses an eyesore. My attention was drawn to the graffiti on these walls.

For sex weakness, contact hakim Tara Chand

It seemed a foolish subject to discuss with one's father, so asking questions about the slogan was out of the question. Meanwhile, the train rolled onto the station platform.

The moment I set foot on the platform, the graffiti vanished from my thoughts. I had so many other things and places to look forward to. Kanpur turned out to be a mixed bag of new and clean localities; old, filthy, fly-infested areas with open drains and dirty children. These were the areas where hoodlums roamed around in the streets, armed with knives with nine inch-long blades and poisoned tips. The newer localities made one wonder if this was really Kanpur. But no matter which part of Kanpur one went to one could not miss these walls with slogans painted on them.

"Shan say dekho, gadha peshab kar raha hai!"

Many years later, I had a chance to see such slogans. It was in Nigeria in 1982 where I was recruited by the Government of the State of Kwara, as a Senior Medical Officer in Kwara State College of Technology in a town called Illorin. In Nigeria, you could change religious beliefs back and forth. The messages on the hoardings in Illorin, the city I lived in, as in the rest of Nigeria, were ambiguous and would not make sense till read in sequence.

For instance, a billboard would read:

HE IS COMING!

When one went further down the road, another hoarding would say:

I HAVE SEEN HIM. HE IS HERE!

A short distance later another one would display:

ARE YOU READY?

There were still others to follow:

I AM! ARE YOU?

And then the final one would read:

JESUS HAS ARRIVED!! BE READY FOR HIM!

Finally, the message was clear!

It was in Kanpur that I came across SaMule. I noticed him standing in a corner watching proceedings of the city with great disdain. He had the most intelligent face, almost like that of a sage. And with my fantasy of a twelve-year-old, I thought he was very handsome too. We were watching a gruesome battle between two human beings who were fighting against each other with bricks. Suddenly, one of them took out a contraption which he flicked open to reveal the largest knife blade I had ever seen. I had never seen knives of that kind. I was used to kitchen knives only. He then pushed the knife into the other man's belly with an angular thrust from the right and dragged it out the left side, opening his abdomen. His entrails and blood gushed out. I have never been very comfortable at the sight of blood. I felt weak in the legs though I did not know why. And then, I threw up. I felt miserable. So, why was I there? It wasn't my fault. I was just passing by on my bicycle trying to beat the sun, which was in such a tearing hurry to call it a day. Suddenly, the two men had emerged from thin air and went after one another. SaMule uttered some words, "What a waste, what a waste!" I found him looking at me somberly as I finished cleaning my face and said, "See you sometime!" Then, I left. I met him many years later in Chandigarh and that is when we became good friends.

While growing up in Kanpur, I formed impressions about India and the Indians.

In my opinion,

- Only the lucky ones are were born in Bharat which was the greatest country in the world.
- Our spiritual masters had made the gift of spirituality available to the whole world.
- Indian women were the most beautiful women in the world.
- Gandhiji's ideas and ideals of ahimsa and nonviolence seemed to me to be the most noble as also the most powerful virtues.
- The Indians were totally non-violent.
- Despite the non violence, Mahatma Gandhi succeeded in throwing out the British from our country.
- Pandit Jawahar Lal Nehru would go down in history as the finest prime minister of India. A respected world leader, he was one of the most educated politicians of India who could speak flawless

English and could do head-stand as well. He loved children, hence his birthday is celebrated as Children's Day.

- He loved his daughter because I had known no other father who wrote such lengthy letters to his daughter, even if he was in jail.
- Our presidents have been illustrious men like Dr. Rajendra Prasad and Sarvpalli Radha Krishnan whose birthday is celebrated as Teachers' Day.

It was around this time in 1962 that China decided to end the "Hindi Chini bhai bhai" façade. They attacked India. It was 15 years after our Independence and the Chinese caught us unawares. The Chinese were hugely superior in terms of weapons, number and the determination to complete what they had set out to accomplish. The Indian army was ill-equipped to fight a war in the snow clad mountains with 303 rifles and gear unsuitable for that terrain. The mortality in the Indian side was very high. I do not remember how the war was brought to an end at that point of time, for I was too young and our exposure to war was restricted to blackouts and patriotic songs. My father loaded planes with supplies for the army. Although now I know that the war came to an end because the Chinese called it off unilaterally.

Chetan Anand made the first Indian war movie Haqeekat, which had Dharmendra and Priya Rajvansh in lead roles. The movie was a blockbuster. Priya Rajvansh was arguably the most beautiful lady I had seen. Little did I know then as a 16 year old that I would become one of her best friends 36 years later in Chandigarh where she had a mansion in Sector 5. The beautiful actor was strangled to death in Mumbai a few years ago.

After the war, Indians lunged for in patriotism. India's melody queen, Lata Mangeshkar, sang a nationalistic song which became an instant hit. Pandit Jawahar Lal Nehru, lovingly called Panditji by the Indian masses and Chacha Nehru by the children of India, was present in the function when the singer sang the song. The lyrics of the song were:

Aey merey vatan key logon
Jara aank mein bhar lo pani
Jo shahid huey hain unki
Jara yaad karo kurbani
Jai Hind, Jai Hind!

I remember that Panditji had shed tears during the rendition of the song and later told the singer, "Beti(daughter), you have made me cry!" it seemed so ironic. *The thousands who died on the battlefront did not bring in the tears but the song did.* And then, in the year 1964, Panditji passed away. I recollect Jasdev Singh was the commentator on All India Radio commentating the prime minister's death, funeral and the country's mourning. Pandit Nehru's daughter Mrs Indira Gandhi threw some flowers on the pyre and her son, Sanjay who had turned 17, lit the pyre. Even Indira Gandhi was not allowed to light her father's pyre. In India, daughters *never* did that. It was traditionally the duty of the sons.

Otherwise, it was believed that the souls of the departed would never reach heaven. That is why sons are so important in the Indian scenario. They are the reason why there are so many Indians in heaven.

The radio was our communication life line. Jasdev Singh was a commentator par excellence. His commentaries on the hockey matches were matchless for their vividness. It was through him that we saw and 'felt' as if we were there, watching the matches! We shouted along with him. We were sad when he was sad at the loss to Pakistan; through him, we 'saw' the Republic Day parades and learnt how great our defense forces were.

My father's next posting was at Pune, although it was still called Poona then. It was a very expensive place even then. On top of that, no one would rent out a place to a person from northern India or a Sikh family in particular. We were non-vegetarians who ate even eggs! Even today, one hears that house owners don't rent their houses to some other communities as well! My father consequently spent a month going all around Poona on a bicycle. The rents were too high for an army officer. The place that he did find finally was a 16 feet by 12 feet room over a garage. It was a makeshift arrangement. The house belonged to Mr. Bhandari who was my father's colleague and he very kindly sublet the room to us. The four of us were supposed to be living in style in a mansion which was a bed room, kitchen, a drawing room and a store, all rolled into one.

We got used to living in that room excepting for the height. The low ceiling made it claustrophobic and my father could not stand straight, for his turban scraped the ceiling if he did. I noticed that the cramped quarters led to short and frayed tempers. All this while, my elder brother was in the National Defence Academy, popularly known as NDA, which was located nearby, at Khadakvasla. Once, I had cycled 16 kilometeres to the NDA and stayed with him for two days, absolutely illegally. I even saw a movie in their fabulous theatre. A couple of seniors decided to make me do front rolls but I was saved somehow.

Finally, we shifted to larger quarters in a suburb of Pune called Kirkee. The officer staying in that house found it too big to handle so he sublet half of it to us. Pune, in 1965, was a haven for those who wanted to study. And I mean really study. It still is. I joined Ferguson College and almost immediately offered myself as a candidate for the post of Secretary for minor games, which included Badminton, (a game which I played fairly well), table tennis, and other minor games. The Maharashtrians were clannish people who would never speak in Hindi or English if there was an outsider in the group. It was all Marathi. In that scenario I foolishly decided to contest the elections against a hardcore Maharashtrian candidate, who apart from being the college table tennis champion, was the local heart throb too. But I won and that too by a huge margin. I had created a record, for no outsider had ever won an election there. And I was all of 16 years of age. That just meant that there were still enough students there who voted for an outsider with guts.

It is a different matter that I could not assume office for my father died of Acute Myeloid Leukaemia on the day the result of the election was declared. He had been ill for only a month. We were soon ready to leave Pune and head for Chandigarh, which was a natural choice, for we had a plot of land in that city. By the way, Pune had no donkeys that I could acquaint myself with in my short stay there.

❑

3

1966-Chandigarh

Chandigarh, in contrast to Kanpur and Pune, was a very modern and clean city in the year 1966. It was a newly developed city nestling between the monsoon streams in the east and north with the Shivalik hills looming large in the backdrop. The hill stations of Simla(christened Shimla later), Kasauli and Dagshai are neatly tucked into the ranges, though on a clear day, Kasauli can be seen very clearly. The roads in Chandigarh were obscenely wide compared to the ones in Kanpur, with hardly any vehicular traffic. The walls too were clean without any graffiti. There were only old people who had decided to come and inhabit this newly laid out city with their children of course after much coaxing by the then Chief Minister of Punjab, Mr Pratap Singh Kairon. Now, *he* was a visionary.

It was commonly said that Chandigarh was a city where

"Harian harian Jhadhian,
Tay chitteyan chittiyan dadhiyan"

(A city of green hedges and elderly people with grey beards).

My friend Har Raj Sidhu added rather jocularly though:

Chandigarh in the late 60's was a city of the tired, retired and the about to be expired!!

This is not really true today because the younger population outnumbers the elderly. The inhabitants of other states had not yet migrated to the city. But subsequently, people from all over the country started arriving in large hordes. This was primarily because of the propaganda in the villages of the states of Uttar Pradesh, Madhya Pradesh and Bihar that Chandigarh was the New York of India. Once they had seen video recordings, the city's enchantment seemed to beckon them, like a beautiful siren. Construction work began on full swing. New buildings started coming up all over town and the people from the states of UP and Bihar left their villages to help build the new city of Chandigarh.

They were not provided dwellings to live in and definitely no place for their ablutions. There was no provision for public utilities. It wasn't their fault. It was the administration which wasn't bothered. So, they used open spaces in the same way as they used them back home. Slowly but surely, the air of the city started changing. Sudden whiffs of unpleasant odour began to pollute the fresh air from the Rose Garden. And one fine day, I noticed a large slogan on a wall which ran thus:

Shan sey dekho, gadhey ka bacha peshab kar raha hai.

Well, why not? After so many years, the next generation of the donkeys had to arrive on the scene doing the same thing that its earlier generation had been berated for. There was a difference here now. I had grown and could understand what the caption really meant. Despite the fact that there were a lot of donkeys in Chandigarh that were used as beasts of burden, it had to be aninsane human urinating against the wall. It was meant to be a deterrent for the person who would thoughtlessly respond to nature's call without caring for the subsequent hardship to the inhabitants of the area. Actually, these people had no homes or shelters. Each one cooked his own food, ate and slept in the corridors of showrooms, In the morning, they used the car parking lots to urinate, the parks to defecate in. They rolled up their beddings and utensils and tucked them in the fork of branches of nearby trees which, over the years, became dedicated to them by default. Subsequently, when   elections were announced, politicians had a master plan up their sleeve. To seek support, these people were allotted hutments! But instead of living in them, they hired them out to new arrivals and continued to live in corridors, although they were now house owners! They sent the money thus earned back to their families in their villages. The new-comers learnt the trick of the trade in a flash and then, they too applied for another dwelling! Politicians in India are most obliging since they see only their vote banks. Walls were available everywhere, so they were convenient. Parks (in the wee hours) continued to be used for other purposes.

India is the only country in the world where the administration encourages people to migrate into overcrowded cities just for the sake of votes, completely overlooking paucity of facilities like sanitation, housing and schooling to name a few. That is the secret why our cities are turning into large toilets. I talked to my friend Stan, who has immigrated to Jersey, USA. Stan has been living in that place for ten years and has not been allowed to bring in his family! People cannot just pack their bags and go to New Jersey for a living. You have to be invited. Politicians do not go around showing videos of that place so that they can get voters in. They have a duty towards the state they live in, hence the strict rules.

Recently, the Chandigarh administration had set up sophisticated toilets for the use of the public. With time, these toilets became filthy, with taps broken and the seats stolen. This is because of complete absence of maintenance and the business acumen of the users to sell off some easily dismountable parts to make money. The number of these people is so huge that the toilets proved to be insufficient and targeted the end users ended up using open spaces as they had always been doing.

It wasn't that the olfactory senses of the authorities had atrophied. They could not do much when their political masters decreed otherwise. They just learnt to close their noses to offensive odors and tiptoed through parks. I met an officer of the administrative services at a function who was deeply involved in most affairs of the city's publicity, and asked him if this wasn't a part of his job too? So that visitors do not go back with the feeling that they have just visited a sophisticated toilet and not the famed city of Chandigarh? His rather prompt reply was, "This aspect of the city's administration comes under the purview of the municipal medical officer! Kindly send your complaint to that department."

He apparently took umbrage to being asked a question in a party because he beat a hasty retreat. Why did he get annoyed? Aren't doctors approached by people with different problems even at parties? Doctors don't mind. Even if they mind, who cares?

It was at that moment when I was reading the graffiti on the wall that I saw a donkey looking at it too. Uncanny it was, but it did seem to me that the donkey was also reading the graffiti. Our eyes met and I felt as if there was something familiar about it. It smiled at me. And then it shocked me by saying, "We have met earlier! We met in Kanpur when the two brutes were slicing each other!"

"Ah!" I exclaimed and asked, "So what brings you here? And how do you manage to talk?"

"Oh! That makes me a little different, doesn't it? I don't do it with everyone, you know. By the way I am SaMule. My master came here in search of work!"

I quickly looked around to see if this funny dialogue between man and beast was being noticed. And before it could get noticed, I needed to get away. I said, "I am Jaideep. See you later." Thus, I left.

Years passed and the message of the graffiti started falling on the retinal blind spots of the one urinating on the wall as well as the passersby. *It was mainly because the person for who the message was put up was illiterate and thus could not read. It is exactly like the slogans on bus stops that you see today:*

Educate Your Children

A slogan such as this is written in English! Ironically, the ones who can read English in modern cities, do educate their children. It is the illiterate ones who need the advice. So, who is reading these slogans? The ones who have already enrolled their children in schools!

Chandigarh, like a giant squid, spread its tentacles in all directions as the number of Sectors rose from 25 to 48 in quick time. The population increased and so did the number of vehicles plying on the roads. The rate of people getting killed in road accidents soared. And so did the stench. While this was happening, the graffiti was generally ignored, not serving any purpose. Moreover, by now the migrants from other states were joined in the onslaught on the walls by the locals. The suffering owners of these building walls experimented with newer and different deterrents till one enterprising individual painted 9 inch by 9 inch pictures of Hindu Gods on their walls. This was a brainwave anticipating that the illiterate masses would not urinate on the pictures of their own gods, thus saving the inhabitants of the building. But the brainwave backfired and the art work was soon painted over. The overpowering urge to empty their bladders won.

There is more to all that stench.

The bare backside squatters next to the railway tracks greet the Shatabadi express as it enters Delhi. Are they to be construed as pieces of art? Looking at what the art form is producing, one could get optimistic about the future of India's green revolution because of the multiple outsourcing of manure from these early morning voluntary organizations, if you would care to call them that.

One could go into raptures, singing emotional patriotic songs! Like the ever green one:

> *"Meri desh ki dharti,*
> *Sona uglay, uglay heeray moti,*
> *Meri desh ki dharti!"*

'The soil of my land where shining gold and gleaming pearls.....'

On seeing these early morning squatters by the side of the railway line, the French President exclaimed, "Aha! No wonder your railways are called La Loo!"

❏

4

Becoming a Doctor
1966-1974

It was time now for me to go to medical school in Simla; it is called Shimla nowadays. I was growing. At a medical school, one learns a lot of things apart from the academics pertaining to medicine, both theory and practice. Firstly, all students stay on the same premises. So, one learns the importance of being united. We learnt how to fight against oppression. Be it from the college authorities or from the local goondas. I remember that we were very fond of our biochemistry teacher. But he was a drunkard. One day, he was charged with molesting his ten-year-old niece who was staying with him. There were a few staff members who were substantiating the charge. But the entire student community was convinced that such an incident could not have taken place in the college premises, with other staff members living closeby. Moreover, the professor had denied all charges. We went on a lightning strike and the teacher was absolved of all charges. After that incident, he was never the same. He taught us but only half-heartedly and for a short time. Later, he tendered his resignation and left.

We, as students had taken a stand and won. And that was more important for us. The teacher was important. **As we went along there were more**

occasions where we proved that medicos always stuck together, irrespective of the validity of the reason. Perhaps it is a similar story in the country's elections where the dumbest people get elected again and again by the majority of fools. Ragging was one of the favored past times. Why should taunting and tormenting a fresher who is already nervous in a new environment and suffering pangs of separation from his dear ones and his roots, give so much pleasure to seniors? But at that point of time, I too was a happy ragger myself. Why did I indulge in it? I really have no answer for it. May be it was the peer effect that I succumbed to so often. I grew out of ragging quite soon. May be, I got bored or then there, was a possibility that ragging began to hurt my sensibilities. Luckily, no one got killed in the ragging process then. Ragging of late has become a cause of many deaths in institutions bringing grief to parents who have pinned great hopes on their children. Now, of course, ragging is being dealt with quite severely, although tragic incidents still occur. Since I could never identify the real reason for ragging, the reason for its continued presence, despite a Supreme Court ruling against it, defies explanation and understanding.

The stint at Shimla was full of fun and frolic. Finally, when we were qualified to be called doctors, we were handed our MBBS degrees in the principal's office. There was no convocation for us. We were not worth it, said the principal. That is a different story. Who cared, as long as we had our degrees to prove our worth.

And then, I was back in Chandigarh. That is where I met SaMule again. It was quite by chance. By then, I had read the book "Celestine Prophesy" by James Redford. The first prophecy says something to the effect nothing ever happens as a coincidence. It was meant to happen. It should not be passed off as a one off chance happening and should be followed up. As a result, I decided that SaMule was not a chance acquaintance and soon we became great friends. I found that he was actually a very intelligent fellow with a fine wit.

I was always very perturbed about SaMule's relatives relieving themselves on walls all over the country. I wanted to know what it was exactly that they had against walls.

"Dr Chadha," said SaMule (of late he had started referring to me as Dr Chadha or doc), "you are well aware of dogs since you have always had them as pets. The male of the species makes it a point to urinate on poles and car tires. You must have noticed the method. It raises its hind leg and lets go of a stream. The females just bend their hind legs and do the same activity. Have you ever seen a donkey pass urine? It *never* raises its leg to urinate. Donkeys are so heavily endowed that it would be virtually impossible to send a stream up a wall. How do you expect my relatives, the donkeys, to urinate on walls? It just isn't possible by any stretch of imagination. But humans have a love-hate relationship with us. They can't do without us and they can't help berating us for any ills that they see in themselves, including a human urinating on walls. They must have a scapegoat, or should I say scape-donkey? If a relative or anyone who is disliked by all and sundry and every one is ashamed of having around, they will denounce him by calling him gadhey ki aulad **(the progeny of donkeys)**. But really, have donkeys ever wronged the human race?"

I replied, "not really. But we give equal importance to the owl too. We call each other *'ullu'* **(owl)** when we are tolerably annoyed with the other party and *'ullo ka patha'* **(offspring of the owl)** when we are very annoyed! Mind you, the owl has never harmed humans in any way either. On the contrary, the owl is a very intelligent creation of God. I think its eyes are responsible for that notion and also because it observes the world without saying much itself. We should learn from the owl. *But if we are angry as hell, we invoke the dog and say, 'Kuttay! Main tera khoon pi jaunga!!'*(Threatening to drink up the other's blood) or *'kuttay! main terey tukadey tukadey kar doonga'* (threatening to chop the other fellow into small pieces). One of our movie stars must have been responsible for quite a few of our country's dogs becoming anaemic and dehydrated. Thank your stars that we are never that angry with donkeys. We have never said, *"uunt ki aulad"* (progeny of the camel). Yes, we say *"hathi ka bacha"* (calf of elephant) if the young person in peevishness is inordinately huge in size and if he reminds us of the jumbo elephant! In certain cases we do call each other *'choohas'* **(mice or rats, depending upon the context)**, if the other party is very timid. If we want to give ourselves credit for something that we are not, we call our progeny *Sher da Puttar!* Even if want to give a genuine compliment to someone, we still bring in the animal kingdom and say, **"You have the heart of a Lion!"** So, SaMule, do you notice how enamored the humans are of the animal kingdom? In fact, I personally think that animals are far superior to humans for they never kill wantonly, nor do they indulge in rioting, and most of all, they never rape! Or even if they do, it is never reported in the local press!"

SaMule asked, "By the way, have you ever seen a donkey passing urine on a wall?"

"Actually, never. They do it anywhere they feel like," I replied.

"I rest my case," he continued haughtily and added, "If the Indian government had been as strict with their populace as the Singaporean government is with theirs (regarding littering, people spitting and urinating in public), the Indian scenario would have been absolutely different. There is a law against littering in Singapore and the punishment is so harsh that no one dare break the law. Imagine what they would do to a person who is caught urinating in public! Indian people respond too but only to harsh measures. The same thing happened under the British rule. There were laws which had very harsh penalties, so no one broke them. You were in Shimla, while studying for your degree in medicine? On the Mall Road in Shimla, the Indians were not allowed when the British sahibs used to out with their families to take a stroll in the evenings. Indians used to be fined if they spitted on the Mall. Of course the British sahibs never spat anywhere. They were thorough gentlemen! They were always well-mannered and well-dressed, hence Indians also had to go out in proper attire, if they wanted to come to the Mall during the day. No pyjamas and dhotis, if you please. And why not? Why can't one be decently attired if one is going out? Donkeys were never expected to follow **those** rules, thank God! A point to be noted here is that every one agreed with the British rules. I was informed by a person who was living in Shimla during the Raj days, that the Mall Road was washed twice a day. Do you seriously believe that they would have let a native spit there. Most probably, this idea did not occur to our freedom fighters, but they should have begun their disobedience movement from Shimla by littering and spitting on the Mall Road. Jokes apart, you humans need is a strict code of conduct and then an authority to make sure that it is followed."

I responded to SaMule's observation, "I wasn't in Shimla during the British rule but even when we were there much later, there were remnants of their rule. There were no rules regarding attire but old habits die hard and the local residents of Shimla apparently had not forgotten and would come out on the Mall all dressed up in their three-piece suits. Was it a force of habit or because they too wanted to just impress the local girls? A rule that is still in force is where everyone is supposed to walk on their own side of the road. The personnel of the Himachal Police still patrol the Mall to enforce that rule. All personnel are at least six feet tall and have to be immaculately attired in their crisp uniforms. The three-piece suits are now vanishing. In our time, no vehicle, except the ambulance, was allowed to ply on the Mall. But now, since the VIPs and VVIPs have started bringing their vehicles on the Mall, the ridge is sinking at a steady pace."

Well! What is the correct definition of a VIP? Who is a VIP? It stands for Very Important Person. But, who is an important person? They have now gone ahead and said VVIP, which means Very Very Important person. VVS Laxman, the cricketer was dubbed Very Very Special Laxman. But, you don't have to be a Laxman for that tag, I am sure.

All these things are relative. Am I not an important person for my patients, for my family and society? And of course, even for myself too. How is a police officer, a judge, a government official or a politician more important than me? Why is there space reserved for them in the car parking area of the railway station, where they do not have to pay only ten rupees for parking their car which could be his private vehicle or he might be using government vehicles for personal use? In the high-way toll tax booths, there is special slip road for these gentlemen so that they can squeeze through the barrier without waiting in queue and without having to pay the tax. Why are they allowed to use official cars even when they are on a personal tour? Why is it that in India there are so many people who must have the tag of a VIP?

But the question still remains — who is a VIP and why? What is their contribution to society which makes them superior to the millions like me? Don't we work? Don't we pay our taxes? Why can't we too go through slip roads without paying the mandatory road tax? Why does an entire city come to a halt when one of our VIP politicians passes through the city? When the prime minister, vice president or the president visit Chandigarh, the entire route is rid of vehicles. The city comes to a stand-still. While in the USA or Great Britain, when their heads of State move out of their home, there is a compulsory wait of only 5 minutes for the cavalcade to pass. When the chief of police of London, who had exhorted the general public not to break speed limits on the TV and print media, gets booked for overspeeding, he gets removed from his post. But in India, as a VIP, he would have the right to go at any speed! On the contrary, our police chief would look stupid if he is not overspeeding.

VVIPs are invited for functions, as if their presence will enhance the value of the function! But really, it does not. What it does is to ensure better press coverage. I am guilty of doing that for one of my book launches. Yes, it did help in the press coverage but then the gains were very transient. On the other hand, when I look back at the launch of another of my books, which was released by the professor of surgery in my alma mater, it turned out to become a best-seller.

Let the VVIPs carry on with the important work they are so handsomely paid for as salary and perks! I have always tried to stay away from events which boast of VVIPs as chief guests. First they expect you to be seated

30-45 minutes ahead of schedule and then, one has to bear the late arrival of the VVIP with his security.

VIPs also have an entourage of security personnel who have no role to play in their security. Chandigarh Golf Club, has many VIPs and ordinary people like us have to suffer their security officials. It is indeed a funny sight when one sees the bodyguard of a golfer holding on to golf clubs in one hand and a few of the man's balls in the other. His gun hangs very innocuously on his shoulder. It is from the security guard's behavior and the golfer's haughty attitude that one can surmise that the person, in addition to being a golfer, is also a VIP. If he had been a VVIP, there would have been three to four haphazardly parked escort vehicles which would have covered the entire parking space.

I heard a humorous anecdote in this context.

There was once a VIP, on the Chandigarh golf course, with his brood of security personnel. A monkey, wanting to see a good shot off the tee strayed within ten feet of the VIP and sat down calmly, waiting for the shot. The VIP hid behind his four ball member and shouted to his guard "Kill it, kill it!" The guard took out his service revolver, took aim and let loose a few shots. Now the monkey had no idea if the thing was a revolver, a putter or a toy. So it just continued to sit there, looking impassively at the golfers with bullets whizzing past it. In the end, when nothing spectacular happened, it just walked off! So much for security! He could not hit a large monkey from a distance of 10 feet!

My friend, Amar Grewal was amused when I told him about the book I was writing. "Remember Squire, when the four ball of tired and retired inspector generals of police was playing the ninth? At the corner of the old zoo where you have the dog leg, they were attacked by a swarm of angry-as-hell bees? They had eight gunmen with them, two with each IG. When the bees struck, they were not choosy whom they stung. All eight men had run for their lives, but the bees would not leave the VVIPs. Poor old foggies, they could not escape the bees because it was quite a distance to the club house. Ultimately they did reach the club house, puffing and huffing with the effort and the bees in pursuit, attacking some unfortunate people who happened to be in the corridor and the toilets at the time."

"Yes, yes! I remember that incident very well," I said.

"My point is that if the guards could not defend the people whom they were supposed to guard when the attack was only from a swarm of bees, what would they have done if gun toting attackers were firing real bullets with the sole intention of punching holes into the VVIPs?"

" Your guess is as good or bad as mine!" I pointed out and asked, "So, why have them in the first place. They are a liability. In fact the attackers can identify VIPs by the presence of gun-carrying guards."

Grewal responded "Exactly! In Punjab and Chandigarh, the entire police force is out guarding the VIPs." According to a report in the local newspaper, 11,000 police personnel are on VIP duty. That doesn't leave many for the task of state security they were hired for in the first place!"

So, why does every VIP maintain guards? Is it just to let the people around know that he is a VIP? Take the case of the VIP who got his daughter married a few years back. He had to invite so many VIPs according to protocol that the whole parking was dotted with white Ambassador cars with red lights atop them. And each VIP wanted to alight at the entrance of the shamiana. It created so much chaos. The non-VIP mortals like us had to park their cars at least a mile away and walk down to the venue. **We had to do it, for in India, the**

common man has no rights because he has accepted the fact that he is not supposed to have any rights. Exactly in the way that our forefathers accepted the fact that it was their destiny to be slaves to one regime or the other. It would have been sacrilege if I had attempted to drive into the area that day. I would have been shot in all probability or else at least given a sound thrashing by their goons. The fact remains that the VIP who was hosting the occasion wasn't footing the bill. That is a different story. But, if he had been footing the bill, the real shocker would have been the scores of food plates the security guards had used up!

Of course, sooner than later, the VIP will retire. But these VIPs have a clique. When they retire, they get another plum job offer which retains them like a VIP for a few more years. So, if one retires as a chief of the department X, he is made a member of board Y. They amass such powers and prestige through means that are fair and foul. They consider themselves the masters of everything they survey.

SaMule spoke very typically, "Why are the VIPs so much in love with the red light atop their cars? It looks like a festering boil ready to burst and throw out its pus. **Why, if they are so fond of them, each of their cars should have four of the gleaming rotating red lights. Just imagine, from a distance, a collection of these cars would give the impression of an alien attack!**"

"SaMule, don't be a mule!" I carelessly remarked. But he was right. If the red lights somehow give the administrative and police officials a high and boosts their ego, they could be given cars with at least four of such lights per car. Their countrymen are so grateful to them for their services that they do not mind giving them so many cars, chauffeurs and free fuel.

"So, did you finally come to know who the VIP and the VVIP is? Does it stand for "Very Insipid People?" enquired SaMule.

"Who knows? Let me narrate a story to you. The other day, I went to the railway station to pick up my son. I turned into the VIP parking area. Sure enough, there was a policeman who stopped me. "This is the VIP parking area. You can't park your car here." he thundered.

I asked the policeman, "So, you don't think I am a VIP?"

"Well, you are driving your car yourself. Secondly, do you have a title?" asked the policeman?" I wanted to tell him that Abraham Lincoln polished his own shoes and was the President of the USA. But that would have needlessly taxed the poor man's brain, so I let it be.

"Ah! I am a cardiologist. Does that qualify for a title?" I asked.

Now, this policeman had never heard of a cardiologist. So, he looked at me and asked, "Does the person who you wish to pick up possess a title?"

I said "No. But he is a chief officer in the merchant navy!"

It again went over his head.

"I am a doctor. Is that a title?" I tried again.

"Yes, if you say that you are a doctor and you are not lying, you can park your car here in the VIP parking lot! If you are lying, it will be against your own conscience, not mine!" he said and turned away from me in disgust, banishing me from his exalted presence as if to say he had nothing to do with liars."

"I was peeved, but the train was already arriving on the platform. I managed to enter the platform just in time to see my son get off. Ah! So that is who a VIP is. He has to have a 'title'. He has to be a director, a councilor or a politician. But I also came to know that 'Dr' is also a title. I was thrilled that I too can qualify as a VIP. But then someone said that only someone working in the government is a VIP. For all the effort that I put in to acquire my Master's degree in medicine, I would be accorded the VIP status only if the policeman said so. I should have felt good, but for some reason which eludes me, I did not. All said and done, the VIPs are convinced that they are gods on earth."

Neelam, my long time friend arrived. She quipped, "Talking about gods, they say that more gods and holy men have frequented India than any other country in the world." When I was in medical school in Shimla, Neelam was studying in St Bede's College. In the absence of a blood sister, she became my Rakhi sister. **In life, whatever one does not have, one craves for.** And we have been carrying on the Rakhi ritual for the last 40-odd years. I feel this is the next best thing to the real thing.

I remarked, "God knows that Indians have been wronged over the years."

"Yes! And He must have declared that frequent and large delegations of saints be sent to India. Hence, there have been hundreds of spiritually elevated people taking their physical form in India. But, for some reason, known to the saints and God, they have given up that practice of late, because ever since I have been around, one hardly gets to seeing one saint of high spiritual caliber in India," said Neelam wistfully.

"But Indians have now started treating those blessed with the gift of the gab as godmen and saints. This is to satisfy the common man's age-old need of having a personal saint around! And there are so many of them these days. There is a new one added almost every day. TV channels exhibit them and their discourses in ample measure, thanks to their rich followers. We would have otherwise lost out on their thoughts on the broadcasts," I pointed out.

"We don't realize that God has been spending most of His time in India, otherwise a country like ours would have vanished from the earth a long time ago!" she remarked.

"Any one, who thinks that India is a country run by Indians and not by God, is grossly mistaken. India must have the maximum number of devtas and devis, 35 lakhs to be precise and then the gurus, past and modern. Sikhs had ten gurus to guide them through troubled times. Then the tenth Guru, Shri Guru Gobind Singh Ji, decreed that after Him, there would be no gurus and that the Sikhs will have to follow Shri Guru Granth Sahib as their guru, a practice that is followed to date."

"The number of pilgrimage places of the Hindus, Sikhs, Muslims and Christians is pretty large and the number of pilgrims massive. If there are so many people camped in these pilgrimages, one would wonder who is working in and for India, and how is India moving? Half the country is on pilgrimage and the other half is watching cricket!

"But yet the country is working, isn't it? That is why my faith in the divinity that is guiding the country is so unshakable. If all these pilgrims had decided not to go on their pilgrimage, there would have been utter chaos in the country. At least for the duration of the pilgrimage, these millions of pilgrims have something very holy and noble on their minds," I continued even as my sister was all ears.

Then, Neelam quipped, "In the US, if an organization can survive without an employee for a month, it is construed that he is really not required in the organization. Here is India, people are away from their jobs for long periods on one pretext or the other. Some are on study leave, others on medical leave and still others on compassionate leave to look after an aging relative. The medical leave is also for the expectant women. This is covered under maternity leave. Then there is of course the fake medical leave. **At any given point of time in India, a certain proportion of the female work force is expecting, lactating or on maternity leave. So, in a way, the government is fuelling the population explosion. If they had made it their policy that their women employees would get no help from the Government after their first child, probably lesser women would become pregnant.** Then there are the employees who are on LTA (Leave Travel Allowance). This is the forced leave that the employees have to avail, so that they can take their families on a vacation. Moreover, the government pays for their vacation too. It is said that the government employees get stressed, hence they need the annual holidays. As if the rest of India is not stressed! Crores of the common man's tax is spent to de-stress the government servant! Isn't it comical? And then this segment needs perks too. Obviously, we are a rich country.

Neelam spoke with much profundity. "India was such a rich country, from minerals to rich alluvial soil to natural beauty. India could have ruled the world economically. But for the many petty rulers with their own petty thoughts and instead of making their country great, they kept fighting amongst themselves."

When these Kings were not fighting amongst themselves, they were involved in all kinds of vices. Therefore India became an easy target for invaders. The same thing was happening in all parts of the world at that point of time. The British had their own little fiefdoms and kept their infighting a regular feature. The French had their royalty too but they settled their score through a revolution with a little neck snipping of their own. The Russians had their Czars, so they had their own little revolution. But in India, royalty was accepted as divinely ordained and not to be overthrown! They just took it as their fate to be ruled by God's own!" I remarked.

Neelam said, "Yes! The Arabs had the same problem. But they had nature's bounty in the form of crude oil. And they became rich. Because of that, they don't feel subservient to the West and the whites any more. Or perhaps they still do. The money that has poured into the country has made them arrogant. India is now one of the poor countries of the world. If only we had used our gold reserves and wealth in the past we too would also have been rich like the Arabs."

"You are gravely mistaken," I said,. "There was a study conducted in Switzerland which says that India is a poor country with rich Indians. Indians have deposits of more than $ 1400 billion in Swiss banks. We top the charts. The combined wealth stashed in these banks by other countries is less than our loot. There is a move to get back that money but so far the attempts have been unsuccessful. Just imagine, even if we could get just half of the money back to India, a lot of schools, hospital and roads could have been built. That money belongs to India and the citizens of India. There are chances that a lot of that money will go the banks because some stashers must have died. We are not alone. The African countries ran into oil and became rich. But due to rampant corruption most of these countries are bankrupt already. The Siera Leonese had enormous wealth in diamonds. But it did not get them anywhere for they were exploited by the whites. In fact it, was their greed and their backwardness that was exploited.

The Indians, according to mythology, were the most intelligent human beings. Perhaps they stretched their imagination so much that they could imagine themselves flying on Udan Khatolas and flying carpets, possessed atomic weapons when most of the world was inhabited by barbarians. They were highly advanced in the knowledge and practice of the art of telepathy and other modes of spirituality. Slowly, our lofty standards began to deteriorate. **We lost all the qualities mentioned in the Ramayana. We have reached a state where we have to be shown TV commercials which exhort us to wash our hands after going to the bogs!**

In my interaction with people from the state of West Bengal, I realized that they considered Bengalis as people not meant to do physical labour. I sought clarification from my friend, Lily Nandi, from Bengal.

She said, "With the amount of brains at our disposal, it would be unfair if we waste that gift from God and spend our time working as laborers in factories or building roads etc. It is people like Rabindra Nath Tagore and Satyajit Ray that Bengal is full of. Just imagine, if Tagore had been a general manager of a cotton mill, or a laborer slogging it out in a factory, would he have created the fantastic poems that he did? And no general manager of a cotton mill or an ordinary laborer in India has ever won a Nobel Prize!"

I responded to the contention "Yes! I agree with you. That is why most Bengalis are generally having tea when they go to office where they discuss theatre and politics. There are hardly any factories where they would like to work. May be, that is the basis of Nandigram. If there were some farmers from the Punjab in West Bengal, it would have become green."

She became vehement, "Yes, it would have become green alright. Because the only culture prevalent in

Punjab is agriculture! Your music is so loud that one has to have ear plugs to survive. Bengali music on the other hand is so melodious. Bhangra is almost like a battle dance. Dance should be soothing to the eyes. I am wondering why Bhangra is getting so popular with the Indian masses. It is catching on in the West too. Since Bhangra is a violent kind of dance, does it reflect the changing mindset of the masses and their tilt towards violence?"

SaMule, the sage, meanwhile interjected,. "I am confused. Should I be happy or sad at the plight of my relatives in the state of Bengal? If they have no work, who is going to feed them?"

A Bengali friend of mine, Mr Mukherjee, a senior engineer in the Pfizer plant of Chandigarh told me a very interesting fact about Kolkatta (erstwhile Calcutta). Early morning, when people are work bound in general, there are certain people who carry large jars on their shoulders (full of water). They have hundreds of small snakes. Quite a few of our ordinary Bengali brethren are addicted to snakes. For one Rupee, they get a snake bite on their tongue and off they go to work and offices or wherever else. One really does not know how long the high remains but that is their routine. Now, if some one gives you this piece of news, won't you wonder if he was making an April Fool of you in December? That is exactly what I did.

My shock and astonishment left me with eyeballs the size of golf balls! I discussed the story with a few more inhabitants from Calcutta and they all seemed to confirm it. I don't know if that practice still exists or have the intelligent people of Bengal given up that habit.

But the Bengalis are definitely intelligent people. From Rabindra Nath Tagore, who won the Nobel prize for poetry, to so many accomplished personalities in the film and theatre industry, including my favourite Utpal Dutt. There have been doctors par excellence from the state too. Mr Amartya Sen received the Nobel Prize for economics. The only field that they do not excel in now, is industry, where they have to do physical labor. Our very own Ambani family started their textile industry from there and moved off to other places. And, of course, let's not forget the great freedom fighter Netaji Subhash Chandar Bose!

"I hate to burst the bubble," said Neelam, "but Indians are hardly the most intelligent people in the world, Statistically speaking, countries like the USA, UK, Germany, France, Sweden have 270, 101, 76, 49, and 30 Nobel laureates, respectively. However, there are only 5 Indians who have won the Nobel Prize!"

"At least, we figure in the top 21! Pakistan and China are not in that list. We should be proud of these five winners. I agree, we tend to forget the simple fact that the number of these winners is over more than 200 years, in a country with the second largest population in the world."

"May be, the white race was prejudiced," I remarked.

Neelam immediately cut me off, "If countries smaller than the smallest of our states have produced more Nobel laureates, is it not our fault? But we still think that we are the most intelligent of them all. Fine! If we don't put ourselves on that pedestal, who else will? But consider the fact that more than half of India's population is in the states of Uttar Pradesh, Bihar and Madhya Pradesh, where most of their post-graduates do not know how to write their own curriculum vitae'. We happily include doctors and lawyers in this category, half of whom get into professional colleges by merit of money power through the payment of capitation fee."

I couldn't say much in the defense of the famed Indian intelligence. So, I let her carry on. Neelam took off on a different track, "What do you expect from a country where the national past-time is to play a silly gambling game called Tambola? A game where the only exercise that men, women and children get is the hand-eye-ear co-ordination. The person has to hear and decipher a numerical disguised as a fat woman or a naughty man or even two fat majors, quickly, locate the number on the tickets in one's hand and then deftly scratch it out before the next one is called. And in case one can't even do that, and scratches a wrong number and goes up to get one's ticket torn to shreds in front of hundreds of booing people shouting 'bogey!' At the end of it all, everyone is happy with some winning some money."

"At least, the game is family oriented where the father gets to see the family once a week and vice versa." SaMule interjected giving a totally new dimension.

"Well, the British had nothing to do with their time. While Indians slogged as peons and servants in their homes, the army and the police where the native policemen tried to catch and kill their own country men for their colonial masters, the British rulers played polo and cricket. So, they brought this game and croquet to give their wives something to do. The Indians have made Tambola a national game and we play it every Saturday night, Sunday morning, at kitty parties and whereever else you can collect 20-odd people! What a collection of losers we are!" Neelam seemed livid with rage.

And in the context of intelligence, the Indians have hardly contributed to science in a way which has helped humanity. Dr Raman's work and discovery of the Raman effect does not affect my life in any way. The electricity bulb, motor car, aeroplane, train, rocket and bomb have all been invented by other countries. Ninty per cent of Indians do not have access to these facilities.

Recently, Prof Bose was inducted into the hall of fame for invention of wireless transmission. But that is a rare case.

Yet, in the past, Indians were experts in psychology, metaphysics ,spirituality and philosophy. For centuries, when no one knew about the art of communicating through telepathy, some Indians were already masters. These masters transported themselves from one place to the other by breaking up their atomic structure. The rest of the world was busy with science, disregarding these miracles. Indians sages (like Baba Nagendra Nath Bhaduri), were levitating themselves when people from other countries were debating upon the laws of gravity. The western world had more clout and hence Newton's apple was given more importance than a levitating man. Likewise the quantum theory was given more importance than Shri Yogteshwar Giri, the Guru of Paramhansa Yogananda, who could co-exist at two places at the same time .

"So, where are these people today?" wondered Neelam and continued, "These days two persons can't communicate even if they are sitting in front of each other. Everyone is busy talking to someone else on the cell phone instead of interacting with the person sitting opposite him or her. Where has telepathy gone? Talking about levitating, every one is already two feet above his or her level. At least they think they are."

SaMule observed, "Really, India needs heroes. Forty years ago, Squadron Leader Rakesh Sharma went along with the Soviets in a space vehicle, isn't it? He is the country's all-time space hero. Imagine, in a country of millions, bordering on to billions, you can count your heroes on your finger tips. Does that make you the most intelligent race?"

"Intelligence is not restricted to performance and excellence in a particular field of study. It is also how a person uses his or her brains as he or she grows into an adult. After hundreds of years of calling ourselves civilized, we still have to be shown TV advertisements every morning, advising washing of hands after going to the toilet. In the urban slums, one sees mothers cooking food next to heaps of human excreta covered with flies. Sadly, these flies alternate among the child sitting next to the mother, the excreta and the food," SaMule's observations were stark.

For the first time, Sachin Tendulkar appeared in a TV advertisement, advising children to wash their hands before eating. It was called "Operation Handwashing!" In this age we should not be told these things by anyone, least of all, the TV. The basic hygiene lessons should be inculcated by parents at home. But what if the parents are ignorant about these things themselves?

I wanted to prove my point, "We had decided to eat out that night. We stopped at an eatery in Sector 22. There were people sitting in their cars illegally imbibing alcohol along with the chicken which was the speciality of that place. As they finished eating pieces of chicken, they tossed the bones out the window. A couple of men pounced on the bones before the dogs could make it and started chewing upon them. They then waited for some more to be tossed out. They did not bother to clean the mud from the discarded bones. It was pathetic that they had to compete with dogs!"

Neelam took over the reins once again and said animatedly, "So what if a few of us sit at dining tables and eat with forks and knives? So what if some of us eat six meals a day? There are people who don't get to eat even one square meal a day and if they do get that single meal, they eat greedily and hastily. Eating with their filthy hands is hardly of any importance in the larger scheme of existence. **This is what excites people from the West. This is what is new for them. How a man could eat chewed up bones, in the company of dogs.**

They would pay a lot to watch such destitution and they give awards to movies and books like "Slumdog Millionaires" and "The White Tiger"! This is what makes them feel superior to Indians."

"No! Just superior humans," said SaMule.

The fact is that most of the world's poor reside in India. So will we be like this for the next hundred years, eating out of bins with other animals? Why are we still like this?

"Intelligence also revolves around what one does after qualifying as an adult. India was one of the first to be civilized. At least that is what we keep harping about again and again. It could be true. But how come other countries became civilized and we got to be uncivilized? The whole of Europe was supposed to be backward when India was already a civilized country. But subsequently, Europe developed a beautiful network of roads and that has enhanced its infrastructure. China built the Great Wall but had lagged behind in good quality roads. They too realized the importance of roads to be built at the village level. They have managed that to some degree. But India still can't maintain the roads that already exist and roads inside villages are non-existant."

I continued narrating my experience in Nigeria. "Nigeria, in the late nineties, was considered backward by the Indians who went there to work as expatriates. But even the most backward illiterate Nigerian knew the rules of the highway, the expressway and the fact that they were supposed to give the right of passage to pedestrians to cross the road. They did not even require zebra crossings to stop for a pedestrian. Everyone behind the wheel would stop as a courtesy. Even Indians driving on Nigerian roads learnt this basic rule on the very first day they started driving there. In India, no one stops for pedestrians on the zebra line, leave alone elsewhere. But Nigeria too does not have good roads in the interiors of the country."

Ordinary, illiterate Nigerians selling papaya by the roadside on the highway, would wish "Have a safe Journey" to the person who has or hasn't bought their product. How many of us even wish our near and dear ones in such a manner? Once I had a transforming experience in Nigeria. We were driving down to the airport and got caught up in one of the notorious go-slows. A distance of 10 feet could take one a few hours. The traffic is hardly able to crawl. I thought I should ask the driver in the lane next to mine if I was in the right lane. So I rolled down my window and said, "Excuse me, is this the correct road to the airport?"

The driver looked at me with an expression of grave superiority and said, "Mr Singh, (they knew that all turbaned Indians were Singhs!) in Nigeria, a conversation with a stranger starts with "Good Afternoon, Sah! Then we say "I would like your help. Is this the correct road to the airport?" It is only then that one would respond. Now please see if we can get this conversation started in the right manner."

I looked at him and then obediently, I said, "Excuse me sir! Good afternoon to you! I need your help." The Nigerian then directed me to the correct lane and said, "Now, wasn't that better? Good Bye." Off he went, grinning from ear to ear.

Back to Chandigarh and I narrate a recent happening. My friend Surinder, owns Chandigarh Medical Hall, a chemist shop opposite my clinic in Sector 8. He also sells a lot of my books from his counter. He asked me if I was writing a new one. I replied in the affirmative and told him about the title. After some time, he walked into my clinic and said that he wanted to tell me about an incident that he had seen a few days ago. It might help my book, he said.

He can keep an eye on the happenings on the road because of the ideal location of his shop. One day, he noticed an old man trying to cross the road with a load in each hand. Unfortunately, for some reason, this road reminds people of the race course in Monte Carlo without ever having been there. Vehicles zip along at unimaginable speeds. The old man would venture into the road only to hurry back to safer zones. Seeing his predicament, Surinder decided to go and help him cross the road. Before he could reach the old man, a Scorpio, driven by a foreigner, screeched to a halt, diagonally, in the center of the road. This prevented any vehicle from overtaking him. He then courteously signaled to the old man to cross. He waited till the old man had crossed safely and then moved off. He had his family in the Scorpio. Surinder observed that even that person must have been in a hurry to reach somewhere. One foreigner had the decency to stop for an unknown Indian, whereas scores of Indian drivers went past without noticing or helping the old man in his predicament. Why are we like this?

Bunny Sandhawalia, a dear friend who is a great golfer too, had just come back from the UK where he works. He was intently listening to our conversation about traffic. Normally, he doesn't say much but that day he decided to join in, **"See, traffic is a good indicator of the nature or mental state of any society at large because its' members interact on a daily basis, at a primary level with complete strangers. That is the place where you can judge the social courtesy, consideration for others and grace that members of that society have for each other. Disciplined traffic anywhere in the world is directly proportionate to a disciplined society**. Look at countries like the UK and Germany. One look at their traffic and you can safely assume that their populace would be totally disciplined. Look at the chaotic Asian culture. You do not have to pressurize your brain to wonder about their traffic. It will be just that. Absolutely chaotic! There can never be road rage in the UK, Austria, Switzerland or Luxemberg because everyone in that country has so much of self-discipline. Road age is a daily occurrence in countries like India and Pakistan which is a true reflection of their social culture. I can tell you another thing. These countries were badly affected in the two World Wars that they went through. They had to stand in line for hours for rations and many other things. That is where they learnt the fine art of patience. They will wait in line without wanting to jump into the adjacent line if they think that other line is moving faster, like we do in India. You will see them waiting in line in banks, at airports or in traffic jam without making a fuss. In India, we are ready to start a riot!"

Dr Anton Reinfelder, the CEO of Groz-Beckert Asia, was a silent listener. Incidently, I am their factory medical consultant. I asked him what aspect of the German character would he grade as numero uno. He immediately shot back, "Our discipline! The moment you step on German soil, the first thing that you notice is the omnipresent discipline. Hence, we even drive in a particular fashion. While driving at speeds of 250 kms an hour, we can overtake a truck on the autobahn without worrying about what the truck driver is going to do. We know what he is going to do unlike the Indian truck driver. The German truck driver will continue in his own lane and will never be a hazard for other drivers."

I was sheepishly thinking about our own discipline. Would I be talking about it with as much pride as the good doctor was doing?

Dr Anton continued, " In my country, parents are very strict about discipline. They will never let the child behave improperly. If he does something wrong, he will be immediately reprimanded, unlike Indian parents. Later in the child's life, Indian parents will get them fake medical certificates so that they can skip sports or skip school and still later get them fake driving licenses. In Germany, no parent will do that. If he has to do military service, parents, no matter how influential, will not get him a fake medical certificate to get him out of military service. The punishment for indiscipline in any sphere is so harsh that no one wants to do something that will earn him that punishment. It is easier to be disciplined. That is where the discipline comes from. Slowly, it becomes our character!"

The point to notice here is that an Indian, the reckless driver that he is in India, he becomes the best driver when he goes to a country like Oman or Dubai or even Singapore. He follows traffic rules to the T. In countries like the UK or Sweden, he will behave like an angel. He will never drink and drive. But the moment he sets foot on Indian soil, he turns into a speed maniac again, a drunken driver. He will break all the rules in the book. What changes him?"

SaMule, who was listening very attentively, said, "I will tell you what changes him. The rules are the same for a local Omani, a Briton or an Indian. But the fear of being heavily fined or even put behind bars or driving license being revoked puts the fear of God in them. The fine is so heavy that he will not dare to break any of the rules of that country. In the months of Ramzan, chances are that they will put you in a cell and throw away the key. But once back home, they know that they won't have to pay for traffic infringements. A small bribe to a corrupt policeman will look after everything. Even if they are fined, the quantum of the fine is so low that it is almost like chicken feed for the rich and their progeny."

While on the subject of traffic sense, the Municipality tries its best to teach the basics to people who like to drive. It has painted zebra lines at crossings and installed traffic lights with timers. Specific warnings are painted in bold letters that request people not to cross the zebra crossings when lights are red. But the urgency to be punctual is so overpowering and their foot so light on the brake paddle that their vehicle automatically inches ahead only to cross the zebra lines while waiting for the lights to turn green, thereby leaving no safe zone for pedestrians. Why do we do it? Why do we want to squeeze through the orange lights at great speeds, knowing that this is against the law. Don't they realize that the guy on the other side is also a punctual Indian wanting to squeeze through the orange light too? And in any case, what will anyone gain out of saving 120 seconds of one's time while putting the lives of many people at risk, your own life to begin with? But then that is India and intelligent Indians live here.

Recently, the Chief Minister of Delhi, Mrs Shiela Dixit, had begun a campaign on the FM radio. She advised people to drive safely, follow speed limitations; avoid drunken driving. She told them not to use mobiles while driving. She also said that the pedestrians should refrain from crossing the road when the lights were green because what was at stake here was their own life. Just imagine. We need some one to tell us this simple fact of life! It is easy to buy a vehicle in India with the kind of loans that the banks are dying to give. One can get a loan for everything here. Getting a loan for a vehicle is a child's job. Thank God for small mercies. But then children don't need a license in India. Do they? It is up to us how well we can break the laws. Parents, driven by the love of their produce, get them fake driving licenses by bribing officials, using their clout or by touting the tout. The commonest excuse is that they have to go to so many tuitions that it is impossible to commute on bicycles. They waste so much time, they lament.

Just then the cyclist ahead of me suddenly shot out his right arm and turned, just like that. He did not even turn his head to see if there was some one following him. I surmised that he has an eye in his occipital region because of which he has rear vision. With great difficulty, I applied brakes and avoided hitting him. I heaved a sigh of relief and waited till my heart rate normalized and then, I shouted, *"Gadha!* **(donkey!)."**

"See! A man does something wrong and you shout 'gadha'! Is it fair for us?" he asked me with a painful expression on his face.

"Sorry! It was just a reflex; a force of habit. We have been doing this for so long without realizing. I did not mean anything personally to you or your relatives. I agree, I was wrong here. But did you see that? He thought that by sticking his arm out, he had done his duty. The rest was my job. It was up to me to figure out ways to save him by being totally attentive to traffic, keeping my reflexes and the brakes of my car nicely oiled. Had he been hit and died, he would have had a life-time to argue in heaven or hell. But the police and his relatives would have made my life hell, here on earth itself."

One can not blame the common man for being ignorant. The Indians produce a child every 2-3 seconds or may be in less time. By the time one generation is educated to a certain degree so that they do not add to the prevailing chaos, the next generation of ignorant people is ready. This generation has never heard of the fact that we promote ourselves as the oldest civilization of the world or that we taught the rest of the world about good toilet habits. By the time they hear about all the gods and saints who had graced India, they are no longer in a situation to gauge whether they are fictional characters or if they actually existed.

"Your problem is your population," said SaMule.

"Yes, our problem is our population. We produce one child every 2-3 seconds. So these cursed lines have to be expected wherever you go. Even in weddings, the queue is the first hurdle to a happy evening. First, you have to stand in a queue to congratulate the parents or hand over the customary shagun. Quite a few of the guests hand over empty envelopes without their names on it. Then, you join the queue to congratulate the newly married couple. To get a drink you have to jostle shoulders at the bar and the final ignominy is standing in line to get food.

Hundreds of very sophisticated and intelligent people have trained themselves to stand in line for food at a wedding reception. The problem is that you have to stand in queue for food these restaurants too. I had been asked for lunch by my publisher at a Chinese restaurant in Khan Market in Delhi. The waiting time was 2 hours! Probably, the publisher knew that there was no chance of getting a table since he was a Delhite. May be, the whole exercise was to impress me? As a result, we had to settle for a different place," I averred in a serious mood.

You have to stand in a queue if you have to watch a movie. Just the other day, I counted 19 pyres burning at the cremation ground. The day is not far when one will have to wait in a queue to get burnt on your way to heaven or hell. May be, the jostling of shoulders that we witness in marriages and in places of worship would soon be witnessed in the cremation grounds and we will have to bribe the pandit there for an early cremation of our loved ones. As it is, there is immense shortage of wood in the crematoriums. The middle men at the crematoriums have a scam in operation here too. The contractor for the wood suffer a loss if the electric crematorium functions at its full capacity. Hence they have to pay the persons in-charge of the electric crematorium to make sure that it does not functions properly. Then the wood contractor inflates the rate of wood to cover his losses. We do not hesitate in making money from the dead. Emotion apart, being dead is just a different state of our being. Yes, our problem is our population! You can say that again and again." I said.

"Donkeys are best equipped to produce, as you would have heard and maybe observed. You humans have even made us a laughing stock in that area. Jealousy is a bad trait that you people possess. But if you have noticed, we don't go around producing children like you all do. And we don't have to ask for permission to initiate the act. **After all the self-imposed obstacle courses, like getting married before being allowed to produce legitimate children, you still have the time to produce so many children that you are dying under the burden of your population.**"

"The silver lining in the population issue is that India has the largest work force in the fields of labor, I.T., doctors and engineers! We also have one of the largest armies in the world today," I said.

"And beggars, criminals, drug addicts and rioters!" said Neelam with contempt.

"Yes," I agreed instantly, the quick rise in numbers has resulted in many things. First and foremost. comes poverty. This is responsible for the lack of education among the masses. There is hardly any food for these people. But the vicious cycle continues. They produce more children to earn more and, in turn, remain uneducated and more hungry. Please believe me. Do not be flattered by the few who have more than they ever require. In no country, are there more homeless, hungry or uneducated people as there are in India. The yardstick for calling a person educated is the ability to sign his or her name. Thus, Kerala is supposed to be 100 per cent educated. What a load of crap! Collectively, the number of people who are drug addicts or who are directly or indirectly involved with crime is highest in India. The number of people in organized begging is the largest in the world. Organized begging is such a huge racket that it is no longer funny. One just cannot escape it. In Mumbai, it is the transvestites. In other major cities, it is the pathetic looking children carrying dirty infants. Then there are pregnant women with one infant in each arm and one in the womb. There are the bandaged beggars, the lame ones and the blind ones! The dons of the organizations of beggars are powerful people who make millions from these poor people. People with soft hearts want to help these beggars without realizing that the alms that they so generously give do not stay with the beggar. It goes to the don who, in turn, gives a dime or two to the one who has earned it. These beggers stand throughout the day in the sun or rain, pretending to be blind, lame or injured, although some of them are actually blinded or amputated by the don's home-grown doctors. Just looking at them masquerading, one wants to shout at the Amitabh Bachans and Shah Rukhs to move over. The real actors have arrived."

If we are so intelligent, how come we have the largest number of organized riots that affect any country in the world. How does such a large mass of humanity succumb to the histrionics of a few and start killing human beings who they have never seen before or who have never harmed them in any way? How come educated and rich people have the audacity to happily steal whatever they can lay their hands on during a riot? It happened in Gujarat recently. Normally, it is said that riots are engineered for the benefit of the have-nots so that they could steal what they did not possess. But here, people came in their cars to pick up stuff from supermarkets that the rioters were busy burning and breaking up. They then rang up their friends on their mobile phones to tell them about the loot that they were leaving behind! This was the year 2002! Every detail was captured on camera.

What makes the ordinary man commit heinous crimes at the bidding of one man or one political party? Is that intelligence? In my book, intelligence would have been to question the decision of the powers that be and do according to what your intelligence and conscience advises you to do. These things happened recently in Bosnia too. They did it to their neighbors with who they had been living peacefully for years! There was one difference though. There was no organized riot in Bosnia.

SaMule decided to give us his opinion, "India was passing through a phase of darkness 500 years ago. Just like the powerful rays of the sun can sometimes be blanketed by a dark cloud, and then it needs a gust of wind to blow it away; similarly in those days, many evolved people had descended on this country to rid it of the dark cloud of ignorance and its' maladies. And indeed, India did prosper much due to these people. But now those dark days have returned and I am sure some gods must be preparing to give you a visit."

Don't we need a divine visit? I thought.

❏

5

Myth: India is an Epitome of Non-violence

The sun had just come out after a short yet sharp shower. I was relaxing in the verandah in my house after a sumptuous helping of rajmah chawal. This combination is dedicated for Monday lunch and it is something I really look forward to. Suddenly, a group of common babblars descended in the lawn and started pecking at the grass, chattering all the while. I wondered what exactly they were looking for. I could not see any worms lying around. They were all so jerky. Every action of theirs was initiated by a jerk. Two of them were sitting on the railing, about eight inches apart. We shall call them Babby1 and Babby2. Suddenly, Babby2 slid towards Babby1 in a flash and with a comical expression, it waited. I waited too. What were they up to? Then, Babby1 turned towards the slider and started ruffling up it's feathers. It dived under it's wings and raised it with it's beak, ruffled some more feathers and quickly jumped up. It ruffled some more feathers. Then, it performed a perfect high jump over the slider, Babby2 and came on to the other side. No one had uttered a word thus far, considering the fact that they are compulsory blabbers. I wondered if a cat had got their tongues. It repeated the procedure on this side and then stopped suddenly. Remember, all their actions started with a jerk and ended with one. Now it just sat next to the slider, touching the slider's body with its own. I looked around at the other magpies and wondered how they could be so happy and peaceful.

Had this been a party of *gabhroo* Punjabis, without any apparent reason (alcohol is just a starter), fisticuffs would have flown all over. Then, some would have swooned, a couple of beer and soda bottles would have been broken on a few heads and iron rods would have made their appearance, Then, baseball bats (which every affluent Punjabi carries), have to be there if the fight has to have some degree of respectability. Finally, to cap it all, knives, swords and a couple of revolvers would have made their appearance out of thin air just. Police would have arrived after everything would be over and they would have demanded their share from both parties. Parents of those involved would have come in their SUVs. Then a few politicians would have made their presence felt with statements to Press and TV reporters. They would have told how peace loving the people involved actually were and that they had been framed by the opposition in order to spoil their matrimonial bio-data. Finally, some sort of compromise would be reached with a covert understanding between the two parties that the issue will be sorted out at a later date.

Indians have always been violent peoples. We have fought ending wars against one another and also, against invadars. We have had a special breed of dacoits in the urban and rural scenarios; we have had riots which would make any human shudder in his bones, we have exploded bombs in trains and in markets, killing innumerable people, we have burnt brides alive and we have killed the female child in her first few hours of life; we have killed our brothers due to greed and we have killed our parents for their property. Now, with the next generation coming in, they kill unknown people against whom they have no grudge, on roads, in their houses and where ever else they can. On the 8th February, 2009, a family of three, consisting of a 35-year0old man, his 30-year-old wife, was killed (along with their 10-year-old son) by a group of boys on the Khanna-Samrala-Chandigarh road. The boys kept hitting their car with their SUV. The car by then was out of control and crashed into a tree. But the boys did not stop hitting them with their car till they were sure that all three of them were dead. They were supposed to be drug addicts. The fault of the man was that he had asked them not to tease a group of girls from a dancing troupe in a wedding! No, I am not insinuating for a moment that we are the only violent people in the world. Humans all over the world have been violent and are violent. More violent than Indians. But that is their problem, not ours.

SaMule said, "If Indians were non-violent people as a whole, crime would be way down. But it isn't. Here again, I take umbrage to the treatment meted out to us. If you humans have to disgrace someone, why don't you do it on your own? No, you have to shoot your guns from our shoulders to deliver the ultimate *coup de grace*. After garlanding your fellow human with shoes and then blackening his face with boot polish, paint or whichever degrading material you may want to use, you load the poor man on to a donkey, to be paraded in the streets. Why a donkey? You could make him walk, take him around in a rickshaw or whatever else you can think of. Anyways, in our meeting we have agreed unanimously that we will continue to behave as we always have....peacefully. We don't want any sort of confrontation with this two legged creation of God. For entertainment, you people catch hold of a 9-year-old girl and lift her by her hair. I agree that it was the parents' fault that they cut her hair so short. The Police Inspector was having such a torrid time trying to get a good hold of the girl's hair. Every one must have hair long enough to provide a good hold for the person who wants to lift them by their hair. The problem is of lice, hence the length of the hair was kept short, no offence meant to the police inspector. This happened on 6th February 2009. You people are so innovative. When you run out of containers, you gouge eyes of suspected thieves and then pour acid into the space thus created. Thank God there are enough thieves around, otherwise you would have turned on each other. When you run out of wood, you burn people alive after raping them under the pretext of riots which justify your religious or political ideologies. Well, that is the way you are trained. We want nothing to do with all that. Human torture chambers are legendary. I just marvel at the brains which conceived them all."

"Torture chambers had their application. If the person under question did not respond favorably, he would be subjected to various kinds of torture so that the interrogator could get helpful answers to riddles bothering them. In war, enemy secrets were pried out of prisoners with the help of imaginative torture," I justified the concept of torture cells.

SaMule carried on, "Like pulling out their nails with pliers and crushing their testicles to name a few of your methods? Most of all, you haven't learnt from the past that these things do not help. Remember what you told me about the war you had with your enemy? To loosen up the tongues of the captured men, your soldiers just crushed the skull of one of them with a huge stone. The brain and tissues which went flying all around convinced the others that a loose tongue was better than a crushed head. If wars, torture and rape were the answer to your problems, your problems should have been over long ago. Are they? Just two weeks ago, we read that in the riots in Bihar, they made the other party eat cow dung and drink cow urine as a prerequisite to their rebirth as Hindus. Ah! You forget so quickly! That is why they stopped being Hindus in the first place! Now when they don't want to be part of your religion, you force them to come back with offerings of bovine excreta! Give me a break! "

"But I must tell you that one of our Prime ministers happily drank his urine everyday to keep his body toxin-free. Osho tells us about a disciple of Mahatma Gandhi. Professor Bansali, a professor in a university, who ate cow dung and drank the holy cow's urine for six months. Note that Mahatma Gandhi declared him a spiritual saint!

"I wonder if that good professor put in salt or sugar to change the taste a bit?" said SaMule., snorting.

This brings us back to the whole concept of Gandhigiri. Is that what we are missing? Is that what we have forgotten? Will Gandhigiri take us away from violence? I have a feeling that it might not succeed in this situation. Gandhigiri was against a rule, against an ideology. Gandhiji had decided not to retaliate against force with force. But here, there is no single, common enemy. We have a class of people, a minority and a majority. Both have an ego problem. Followers of the principle of Gandhigiri have been fighting against the corrupt. So far they have failed.

Who do we organize a non-violent movement against? First, we have to realize that we have a fight on our hands. The realization that the fight is with our own selves comes next. Once that happens, there are chances that we might succeed. We have to fight the lawlessness that has crept into our souls. We have to fight the violence that has pervaded into us; we have to realize that there is no valor here; that there is no pride in these senseless acts. This is not the way to show our independence. Independence also means that we proudly take responsibility of our actions. It is not just the profession that one is in. What is more important is the thought process in the individual's mind.

I'll illustrate this with the help of a story. Once upon a time, there was a prostitute who lived next to a temple. The priest was a middle aged man who was very curious about her. After his duties, he would peep at her and wonder about her nocturnal activities. She excited him and his imagination would run a riot, literally. The prostitute on the other hand, would finish her early morning chores and look towards the temple. She was banned from entering it. She would wonder about the priest as to how lucky he was since he was with God all the time. He was spending his days in the service of the one with whom she had very little contact because of what she did. She thought of the pure thoughts the priest might be having, being so close to God! She was oblivious to the thoughts of the priest and how much she was in them and how!

One day, they both died. The prostitute found herself in heaven and when she looked down, she saw the priest languishing in hell.

She became very upset and rushed to God and said, "Dear God, there has been a grave mistake. I should have been in hell and the good priest should have been in heaven!"

God replied, "There was no mistake. The priest had a good, clean and pious job. But he had very impure thoughts about you and your profession. So he earned a place in hell. You, on the other hand were in a profession which was considered low but your thoughts were very pious. You earned your rightful place in heaven."

One might be a doctor or a teacher and have unholy thoughts about his patients and pupils. They have no right to be in those professions. The argument had begun with the why? Why, after so many years of our existence as a country, have we degraded to such levels? This will require some introspection as we go on looking at some of our other idiosyncrasies. If you see the history of countries like the United Kingdom, the USA, and the Scandinavian countries, you would learn that they were barbaric. How come they became so sophisticated and suave in such a short time whereas we have gone from bad to worse? One man, Mahatma Gandhi decided to experiment with a new mode of protest. It was termed as Non-Violence. But they killed him in the end. Death and killing are always violent. May be, he had outlived his utility? One is not sure if we learnt this from the corporate sector or the corporate sector learned this from the politicians. Once a person out lives his or her utility, he is asked to leave. The method of removal differs in politics, where the end can be very violent.

"Boy!" said SaMule and added, "He should have thanked his stars that he was nowhere near Uganda when His Highness Idi Amin was busy bludgeoning his political prisoners to death. To save on bullets, he asked his prisoners to bludgeon each other till blood was ankle-deep in the room. Had Mahatma Gandhi decided to use his Non Violence movement in Uganda at that time, Idi Amin would have been overjoyed, if not ecstatic. I really can't explain the British behavior; it is totally enigmatic. At one end of the spectrum, they heroically shot 60 Kuka Sikhs from the open end of their cannons and hung them by the scores and then go on to merrily shoot hundreds of innocent people in the Jallianwalla Bagh and at the other end, they can't get rid of a frail old man. Were they scared that his death would trigger off a violent Indian uprising which they would not be able to handle? Strangely enough, the Indian masses did not react to the killings I mention. In India, people don't retaliate because a leader, no matter how dear, is killed. They make martyrs out of them. Indians retaliate if a pig's head is found in a mosque or a cow is slaughtered in a temple. They retaliate if their cricketing hero is given out and the commentator confirms the wrong decision. They did not retaliate because Mrs Indira Gandhi was killed. They organized the so called 'retaliation' because it suited their political cause. They don't retaliate if they don't have food on the table. They retaliate if their OBC status is taken away from them." He stopped talking for some time and looked at me for an answer. When there was nothing forthcoming, he carried on.

"The other day, there was an anti-helmet demonstration at the Matka Chowk of Chandigarh by a few Sikh women. They held the helmet to be against the tenets of Sikhism and in any case, they did not need helmets because their skulls were very hard. I am not saying that they were right in their assumptions. Any head can be crushed under a truck. But to prove this point, a coconut was placed on the heads of some volunteering women. Blind-folded men shattered the coconuts into smithereens through lathi blows! And after the demonstration, the women stood up happily, demonstrating how tough they were. But in the Dandi March , each and every volunteer swooned and fell to the ground after the blow which was half as powerful as the one which shattered the coconut on the heads of the Sikh women!"

SaMule couldn't wait for me to answer. So, he continued, "Now why were the policemen Indians? Did they not have enough to eat in their homes honorably? Or was it that they had reached the depth of depravity that they had to work for the invaders and rain blows on their own country men? **I feel that the British had stayed in India for so long that successive generations of Indians had succeeded in brainwashing themselves(if they had any brains, that is) that the country basically belonged to the British and they were there just to serve them as their slaves.** Why couldn't Gandhiji convince the slaves working for the British in their offices and homes to leave the service of the British and join freedom fighters in their struggle for freedom? Who was the leader of these people? And why were they so adamantly loyal to their white masters? There were so many of your countrymen working in the army, in civil offices and in the police. They were even spying on their own countrymen for the British. Jailors, who committed atrocities on Indian prisoners were also Indian. The truth remains that Indians have been the greatest sycophants the world has ever seen. Not that other countries do not have their share of sycophants. Every country has that breed. But imagine, while your own countrymen are fighting to dislodge the invaders, you are working for the very people who have enslaved your country. And you have the temerity to rain lathi blows and bullets on them."

The Gurkhas had fired on people in the Jallianwalla massacre. Why blame General Dyer? He just gave an order. Had even one of those Gurkha soldiers turned his gun on him, instead of his own countrymen, the whole story would have ended there itself. Army discipline, my foot! What happened to the Gurkhas? Were they blind? Could they not see women dying, couldn't they see children covered in blood? Couldn't they see old and lame people running for their lives and jumping into wells? Couldn't they hear the screams of the wounded being trampled upon? Had they suddenly begun to think of themselves as more British than the British? After it was all over, did they feel proud of what they had done? Are their progeny proud of the actions of their forefathers?

I said, "Yes, the French, Yugoslavs and Poles did not work for the German occupation army. They constituted underground forces which fought them at every level. That is how they maintained their pride and achieved freedom in a short time. On the contrary, their Indian counterparts even fought for the British against other countries and their own countrymen for the benefit of British interests. The worst thing was that they were proud of what they were doing. Ironically, they had very little pride left in them. The little that they had left was dedicated to the fact that they were working for the white sahib. Years later, Indians, who were remnants of that era, praised the British to heaven and back. They swore by them! Why would they do it? Were they blind to the fact that there were other Indians who were trying to throw them out and getting killed in the bargain? If fighting in the British Indian Army, as it was called, was so important to the Indian cause, Bhagat Singh and his friends would have been at the forefront, slogging it out! But they were not!"

SaMuel continued, "Come on Dr.Chadha. The British, in those days, were a breed apart. They were mostly satisfied with what they were paid. Their perks made up for everything else. Most of the British sahibs, as they were called, were very proud people. Proud of their King and proud of their country. What they did was for their country. That is where the pride comes from. Look what your Indian people have been doing after they achieved their so-called independence. Everyone has been looking out for himself and for his family. I am sure the sycophants in our country will make sure that the next Prime Minister of the country will also be from that lineage. For us, it is natural justice. They could be right in doing that because, apparently there is no one else in the country who is prime ministerial material. Don't look at me. We don't have any interest in forming governments and we don't have any idea who our children are and where they go. Hence there is no clash of interests."

I met Mr Pishora Singh and since he had been born during the Raj days, I decided to ask him about what he thought of the Indians in those days. His opinion was different. He said, "The ICS was the civil services in those days which became the IAS of today. The man who made it to the ICS was a man of honor. He used to be a man who would do his duty honestly and completely, without prejudice. Compare the government officers of today. Can any one say that they do their job with honor? Does every officer come from a rich background? Rich enough that he can send his children abroad for further studies? Look around and see the number of the children of the officers of government who are studying abroad. Dirty money is being paid abroad. They have houses in the best localities of top cities of India. They have houses all over the world. The Punjab Government recently came out with a list of tainted senior administration officers!

The public knew about them much before the police or government. Where is the list now? You must be wondering how they must be surviving the calamity that fell on their cushy lives? I will tell you. No such calamity felled them down. They are still working on their coveted posts! Because they look after their own!" Our very own, the Chief Minister, chided his fellow politicians the other day and said "You should learn from these officers. They look after their own, whereas we in politics, turn against each other at the first opportunity."

I knew an officer who would drink a whole bottle of whisky. One day, while we were sipping beer after a round of golf in the sweltering heat, I was shocked to see his driver balance his sandals on the palm of his hand and walk regally into the club house. He sat down at his master's feet, untied his golf shoes, put on the sandals that he had brought along, raised him up and literally carried the officer out of the club. This man would not have had the guts to even touch his master the next day! Neither would the officer have let him. So when I told some friends about this event, they just shrugged it off by saying that it was a daily occurrence!

"So, was the white sahib better or is today's sahib better?" Mr Pishora Singh asked.

I put forward my feeble argument that at least, this one was an Indian. The slavery issue is in our genes. But we are slaves by choice now!"

"I tell you. As bosses, they were far better than the ones we have. The Indian bosses have no honor. They have no pride. They have no self-respect. They are like ostriches. They think no one sees them, thus whatever they do is not known to the ordinary man. But everyone looks the other way and carries on their sycophantic activities. Because no one has the guts to drag them out of their plush offices and demand to know what they do with public money, who sends them abroad and why and who sends their children abroad to study. The courts have rightly ruled that the spouse of the corrupt officer should also be charged since she has been enjoying the fruits of her husband's treachery towards the nation. The problem is that there is no system of instant justice. The cases drag on for years, be it rape, murder, embezzlement or passing national secrets to a foreign country. Hence there is no accountability for any crime. The criminal happily goes on doing what he has been doing. In fact he does it because he knows that he will never be accountable for any of his deeds."

We agree that the British were good as bosses. But that does not exonerate the Indians from the blame of being sycophants. Subsequent generations of Indians have been brainwashed by politicians into believing what a great job the Indians of that era did in getting us our independence. All of two hundred years, it took them! All the while, their predecessors were hobnobbing and partying with the British and in return the British patted them on the head as if they were their pets, which in fact they were. **I for one am ashamed of people of that era. They were the ones who made us loose it in the first place and then helped the enemy to maintain its' strangle hold on our country for so long.** In fact, we were already so used to slavery when the British arrived that it that we immediately accepted it as our lot. The Mughuls had made our forefathers used to being slaves. They learned how to do 'salaam' to the Mughals to perfection and then, they graduated to doing that to the British! There must have been endless generations of Indians who were born into slavery, thus they knew nothing better.

We certainly were masters in the art of being good slaves.

When we were not being ruled by outsiders, we were being ruled by our own so called Rajas. Pride was an emotion totally alien to the psyche of our ancestors. Hence they just shifted gears and graduated into the caste system where they were slaves to a different set of people. The only difference was that new rulers were also Indians.

It was a situation of slavery within slavery. While Indians were enslaved by various invaders, a parallel internal process of slavery of the infamous caste system was in full flow. The Brahmins had the audacity to call themselves superior to the sect they called Shudras at that time. It was a joke. How can a slave call himself superior to another slave? The ones, who were looked down upon as untouchables, agreed to be that and agreed to carry out that role to perfection. They did the menial job not for a day, not for a few years but for centuries! How can hundreds and thousands of people agree to the humiliation of that degree? And that too against a few people professing to be from a superior class of human beings. They were ready to work as scavengers, carriers of the night soil! Were they animals or what?

Slavery in India did not end with the departure of the British from India. It was as if we were not fully satiated by 200 years of slavery. We wanted more. So we went to England to work for them as laborers, sweepers, doctors, engineers and taxi drivers. We did those jobs in England which were below the dignity of ordinary British citizens. We were ridiculed, looked down upon, subjected to racial discrimination but we still wanted to serve the crown and sing songs glorifying the Queen of England. Why? Was it only because of the money? Or, was it because being associated with the white skin is so important to us. After so many years of winning our so-called independence, the British still blame the Indians for dirtying their neighborhood. So what if an apology is issued later? The damage has already been done.

After serving the British health system for so many years, Indian doctors were on the verge of being kicked out of that country — so much for gratitude. I agree that these people cannot come back because they might not get jobs which are equally well paid to help them maintain the standard of living that they were used to in England. But the fact still remains that the generations of today are still clamoring to go and work in the UK. So bad is this craving that a particular Gurdwara in Punjab has a room full of airplanes which have been given by the devotees to appease the Guru so that He listens to their prayers and flies them to a foreign country!

As I walked down the road, I was hailed by my friend sitting in a huge vehicle. He was beaming from ear to ear and shouted "Doc! My son has got a job in London!"

Now this friend of mine has a thriving business. He is a contractor and by knowledgeable guesswork, has a decent amount of money. He owns many more luxury cars like the one he was sitting in. It was obvious that his son does not want to carry on the family business and wants a life in the finance sector. Since the writing of this book loomed large on my brain at that point of time, I blurted out, "It took

Indians 200 years to quit being slaves to the British and you are so happy that your son has revived that tradition of working for them!"

"Do you know how good they are in finance?" he asked.

"Congratulations! They are on the verge of bankruptcy. In any case they never had anything of their own. They have been stealing from the world ever since I can remember," I said and walked off.

I was upset, though I had no reason to be upset over an issue that did not concern me, directly or indirectly. While conducting a medical examination for a Merchant Navy Officer, I asked him where he got his ticket from.

"U.K.!" he replied.

"Is U.K. racial?"

"In a recent survey, U.K. was adjudged the number one racist country in the world. America was last, even better than India. Yes sir! It is racial!"

"So why didn't you get your ticket from India?"

"Whoo! It is really tough here, Sir! The guy taking your examination might fail you without asking you even one question." I was aware of that, so I withheld my comments.

"But in the UK, they encourage people from other parts of the world to come and get their tickets. There are bright chances that one can pass in the first attempt, whereas in India it is a rarity!" I believe things have changed now. Passing from UK is no longer a piece of cake."

"We have nothing to do with the Merchant Navy or the finance sector. We are slaves too. We are slaves to the Indian washer-man and the contractor. He gives us food and shelter and as you know, since our needs are few, we don't crib and we don't expect any more. But in your case, yes, you might be right. The French don't work for the English. They have their grudges. Maybe, you Indians are like us. You have no ego, which is a good thing. Most of you have forgotten your past and you just look towards your future. And if it is secure in England, so be it. You have to work somewhere and if the pay is better in England, then England it is."

During the British rule in India, there were some Indians who belonged to a generation which came after the one which was already working for them. They had no idea what slavery was but found themselves born in this awkward situation. They decided to take it upon themselves to get liberated. Thus a whole new set of proud Indians was born and in them, were the likes of Bhagat Singh, Uddham Singh, Rajguru and his group. It is to them and their likes that we are indebted and eternally grateful. Despite the fact that Udham Singh went all the way to England to kill General Dyer but ended up killing Mr Michael O'Dyer, the Governor of Punjab! That was a case of mistaken identity while the original intended victim General Dyer took grave umbrage.

Never should the liberty of our country be in the hands of traitors. Traitors who sell the countries' secrets, buy sub-standard weapons and supply sub-standard equipment for our brave soldiers.

But that does not mean that Indians were non-violent to begin with or they became non violent just because Gandhiji told them to stay away from violence. We have been killing all and sundry ever since the country came into existence. We have been fighting wars with invaders, with each other and finally the British. It did not end there. We have had wars with the Pakistanis and the Chinese, never mind who started them. The Indians fought with courage and grit. There was no question of preaching the theory of non-violence to an invader or the rioter. The theory of non-violence never existed anywhere in the world, least of all in India. Violence is in our blood right from the days of the Angulimal, who later became Maharishi Valmiki, down to today, where Indians have taken it upon themselves to be violent.

Because of our love for cows, who we called our Gau Mata, we became slaves to Mehmood Ghaznavi, who came in with a herd of cows leading his army. Our soldiers ran away from the battle-field and let Ghazani take over and plunder India. Because we were drug addicts, postis and had selfish rulers, we became slaves of the British. If we had kept up the pretence of non violence after the departure of the British, we would also have been slaves to the Pakistanis, the Chinese and whosoever else wanted to throw marbles at us.

Gandhigiri is there only on paper, if it exists at all. I am not sure if anyone would have remembered Gandhiji a few years down the line. In a study conducted amongst the modern generation of the U.K., most thought that Mahatma Gandhi and Winston Churchill were fictional characters. I am sure there must be many in India who think on the same lines. Some must be wondering if Mahatma Gandhi was a modern-day Superman or a Spiderman, who could perform super deeds to push the British out. If he is remembered at all, it is because of the generation which is set to become extinct and the politicians, who revive his memory when it suits them. Sanjay Dutt, in the movie Munna Bhai M.B.B.S, has been instrumental in keeping Mahatma Gandhi in circulation for some more years. In my recent visit to Ahmedabad, I expected to see a lot of Mahatma Gandhi there. But his fleeting presence, came as a surprise to me. In Gandhidham, I did not see even a single dedication to the great man!

The gap between the urban and rural areas is ever widening. The rural sojourn into crime is just waiting to happen if it has not already begun. In the villages of UP, Bihar and MP, it is a reality. In other states, it is under the garb of the Naxalite movement and Bodo movement. At least, these movements want to improve their lot and will not take things lying down. In Punjab, we had militants who had a point to prove. I am still wondering what it was. Gandhigiri is no longer relevant to them, no matter what the political bosses might want them to believe.

The Escalating Violence

One often wonders at the escalating violence in society which includes violence in cities, colleges, homes and on roads. What makes everyone so angry? These days, people kill at the drop of a hat. They do not think about the consequences of their act. The use of guns, sharp-edged weapons, iron rods, bricks and anything else which can be used as a weapon, by the most unlikely offenders is a frightening prospect. The seriousness of the weapon used has no relationship to the seriousness of the reason for the violence. When we were young, violence was the realm of a few gangsters. The common man and students were usually mute spectators. But that did not affect the common man.

Today, the common man or woman is attacked without any reason by unknown people. There is a very thin line dividing a ordinary run-of-the-mill citizen and criminal. Why is this happening? This is not an international trend. This is a trend in our cities involving the rich and their progeny who have access to the powers that be and the lower middle class, who have nothing to loose. As I write, on 30th September, a TV anchor was shot in her head as she was driving home from her office at 3.30 a.m.! She was said to be the friendliest person in the system. Now, why would anyone want to snuff out a young life without a reason? Road rage, enmity, anger, frustration, or was she running from would-be-rapists, or was it just for the fun of it that she was killed? But the end result was that a person could not live her life because of some fools.

I asked my friend SaMule, the donkey, "OK! Let us face it. Have people lost it?"

"To an extent, yes! They have no trust in each other. The mantra is to hit the other guy before he hits you."

"But why should the other guy be so keen to hit you?"

"There is a total lack of trust and patience for each other. But that should ideally happen to a few people. What is happening here is an epidemic of sorts where every one has lost trust and patience for the other person. Parents, by protecting them, encourage their children into these senseless acts of violence. Don't they know that tomorrow their own son could get hurt or even get killed? How will their connections help then? They have no connections with God or do they? Most parents know if their child is up to no good. Instead of correcting the behavior, they laugh it off. Sometimes, when their ward is in deep trouble because of what they have done, they bail them out, sending wrong signals to their children. This is more so in the rich and famous. That is why there are so many cases of high speed cars going over people and killing them.

Or, is it because they do not want to face the fact that as parents, they no longer have any control over their own children. Maybe they are even afraid of them?

SaMule said, "I think young India is going through a reactionary phase. They have now gone into a phase where they think that they are totally liberated, with no fear of authority, bordering belligerence. They think and do as they feel like with no respect for anyone. They want to do everything that their ancestors had been curbed for. Thus they are dabbling with violence at home and in the street, freedom in their expression of sex and traffic violations. But along with this, one can see their aggression in their fields of work and at the office place. In fact they are more alive than they ever were, which is a good thing. This change in attitude is also seen in those people who some years ago were labeled as Untouchables. They are prepared to fight for their rights. They have a will to be at par with the rest of India. One can see rag pickers, rickshaw pullers, street hawkers using mobile phones as if they were born with one. It is indeed a very healthy sign."

Neelam quipped, "I agree that the young Indian is the new emerging macho man. Ideas of fast cars, motor cycles, mobiles and clothes to match come from movies imported from the West. One would think that all parents in urban India are multi millionaires and can easily afford all that their children ask for. That is really not the case. Most parents can't afford these luxuries. So where does the money come from. It is any one's guess. In rural India, things are different. There is hardly any money to pay fees of schools and colleges. Why talk about education? Most farmers in villages are so deep into debt that they have only one answer that satisfies everyone... suicide.

To stop these incidents of suicide, the Government has recently coughed up 1000 crore Rupees to help them. But I doubt that this gesture will help any one. Don't we have the modern Indian cannibals who will devour the money and let the poor farmers continue to commit suicide? Have we forgotten the Tsunami? When help was pouring in from the world, our own cannibals were busy gobbling up the money and food coupons meant for the suffering masses. Shouldn't these people be shot in the market square??"

Our Past

We Indians have short memory; be it the partition of India and the subsequent killings, political blunders, or the losses and disasters in a sport. Very few from the modern generation remember the reason behind the partition of India. Our elders, who were there in the Raj days, were so happy at being treated so well by the British. All that they did not say was "Sit, Tommy," come here, Tommy or may be they did. I don't know. I wasn't there. In a country that was ours, our ancestors were so obsessed by the white sahib, that they forgot that there were clubs in India which had boards on the main gate proclaiming :

"Dogs and Indians not allowed!" and that too in our own country!

Our glorified politicians, who were so busy getting anglicized that they had no time to prevail upon their highly placed contacts to remove the vicious boards from the clubs of Calcutta. Or did those boards fall on their retinal blind spots too. Or maybe, they did not care, for they were so deeply engrossed in themselves. The rest of the eye was of course only for the white women; mesmerized by the ladies saying," Look! How English this native has become. He is such a pooch!"

Exactly in the way we react if our dog stands on its hind legs and attempts to walk a bit. Only difference is that we don't have affairs with our pets. The British were more magnanimous than the Indian.

We promptly forgot all that the British did to our self respect or the lack of it. The generations that came later on did not want to remember the 'Raj Days' as they were called. They had nothing against the British. What happened at Jallianwalla Bagh in Amritsar seemed like a bad dream and it had happened not to Indians but to some one else; some one else in some state called Punjab, God only knows where it is! All the hangings were done and over with. The fact that the Kuka Sikhs were tied to cannons and blasted did not matter to Indians any more.

Since I am a Sikh, I wanted to know about the contribution of Sikhs in the struggle for independence. I was impressed, never mind the few small time Rajas of the state who were known for their sycophancy. In the first war of independence in 1857, more than 250 Sikh soldiers were pushed together in a small enclosure where most of them died by asphyxiation and the survivors were shot in the morning. From 1857 to 1947, 121 freedom fighters were hanged, out of which 93 were Sikhs. Another 2600 were sent to the Andaman islands, out of which 2350 were Sikhs, 66 were blown by shells; all 66 were Kuka Sikhs. The property of 2600 hundred freedom fighters was confiscated; 2300 of them were Sikhs. All from the state of Punjab! This information in no way belittles the contribution towards the country's independence by Indians from other states of India."

My boss in Nigeria was a Polish lady doctor who was three years old when Hitler invaded Poland. No matter how much I asked her about those days, about the Germans, the Jews (Juden, Juden! I would try to jog her memory), the concentration camps, I hit a blank wall of absolute amnesia. She had no idea about the War days, German occupation, the killings in the concentration camp or the gas chambers. Thus, she claimed brilliant ignorance. I wondered why? May be, the Poles of her generation did not want to remember the ignominy of days goneby. They wanted to just forget the past and get on with life. They did not have independence day celebrations as we do!

There must be a Pollywood of some kind in Poland too, where film directors make films about the heroic Polish underground fighters, just like they do in India, thanks to producers of Bollywood film. These films which take us back through the days of partition and the horrors of the killings of those times. Mr Khushwant Singh, the famous Indian author, did try jogging a few memories in his book *Train to Pakistan*, but that still hasn't affected our younger generations. Most of them haven't even read it. Some might have watched the movie.

Wonder of wonders, they still want to go and study in England, suffer the racial abuse and work for the British, and get their names changed to Harry for Harinder Singh and Joe for Joginder Singh and Sam for Subramaniam, all because the inhabitants of that country can't pronounce Indian names. Now, isn't that funny? And when they visit India for sabbatical, they continue to think that their names are Sam, Harry and Joe. But the French don't forget their past relations with the British and refuse to even converse in English. Why is there is such a vast difference in behaviors?

The French, Yugoslavs and rest of the world, which had been plundered by the Germans, except the Italians under Mussolini, refused to help or work for the Germans. On the contrary, they had formed underground groups which fought against the German army by sabotage. Mussolini thought that by acting as a stooge of the Germans, he too would become a superior German. But look at the way he died and how his body was abused by Italians themselves. For those of you who don't know, they hung his body in the street and every passing person spat on his dead body. On the other hand, Indians worked in offices, railways, the army and as peons and servants of the British occupying forces. Not only that, they were **happy** doing their bidding. And no one spat at them. If only some of our ancestors had done that, some Indians would have stopped working for the British. No doubt, there were some of our countrymen who were fighting against the British but in a disorganized manner. Why? Didn't they realize that there were some Indians, like Netaji Subhash Chander Bose, Lokmanya Tilak, Mahatma Gandhi and the young brigade of Bhagat singh, Uddham Singh and their friends, who were trying to kick them out? Today, when it is again our own India and ruled by Indians, we declare bundhs at every conceivable triviality and bring the country to a standstill causing huge losses to the country and people. Why didn't we declare bundhs when we were being ruled by the British? Why didn't they have pen down strikes? Why didn't they dessert the army and go back to their own villages or where ever they came from? The British did not have enough of their own troops to go after them? Why? Doesn't some one have to answer these questions? In the remote corners of the country, there were often only one or two British officers who controlled the entire region. Couldn't our esteemed country men have disposed of those people? No, they did not do that. Instead they took orders from one man and continued to be slaves!"

I said, "But the British did so much for India, didn't they? They constructed roads, installed the base for the largest railway in the world. I am not doubting that Indians could not have done all that by themselves. I am sure we would have. In the post Independence era, we have not only been able to maintain the one we constructed under British supervision, but have also expanded it to make it the world's largest railway. "

The urbanized rich and classy Indians of that time, who were busy with their addictions and self promotion and were hobnobbing with the British, were happily rewarded by their white sahibs with plum postings, land, property, the titles of "Rai Bahadur", 'Sir', and "Rai Sahib." Their wards were sent off to England for further studies. The rest of India was very happy working for the plunderers of the country. While one set of Punjabis was fighting for the liberation of their motherland, there was another set of Punjabi sycophants who were happy with titles and doles that the British threw at them. Incidentally, with rising cost of land these days, the progeny of those Punjabis rule the roost today because of what their ancestors received as dole.

It was the people of UP and Bihar who were up in revolt against the British and refused to work for them. That revolt of 1857 was what shook them and also Mahatma Gandhi's non-violent agitation. Didn't our ancestors realize that the future generations would analyze their behavior which cursed India with more than two hundred years of slavery? For their efforts, we still have the audacity to 'celebrate' independence days proudly, year after year!

Why should we celebrate this day and not forget about the days that India spent in slavery, misery, humiliation and poverty? Why should we remember these days of mourning that they actually are; because this day should never have been there in the history of our country in the first place. How can an alien country rule over another for over 200 years? Isn't it preposterous? Without having an army big enough to control this vast country of ours? Only because the army that they used to subjugate Indians had Indian soldiers in it! And who were most proud to be a part of the invading army; because 'the white sahib' treated them fairly; better than the way they are treated now? What did the great Chanakya have to say about such conditions. After all, most of his theories were relevant in those days. What a pack of donkeys, ah SaMule?" I asked.

"Now, don't start that all over again! Call them a pack of humans, if you please! And accept them at that."

"We are also very happy that Indians are doing well abroad, forgetting that they are a miniscule percentage of the ones back home who have no idea what the phrase "doing well" means. Half of them have never seen the inside of a school, one third goes to school but never get to see teachers. Very few of them get to eat three square meals a day. Never mind the few who eat in the Tajs and the Marriots of India at 2000 to 3000 rupees a meal and don't even care to finish it.

The following set of information was given to me by a person who is in politics and was talking about her constituency in the border area. In the good old state of Punjab, illiteracy is rampant. The most important person in the village is the teacher. **Unfortunately, he also knows it.** He gets 18,000 Rupees for being on the rolls and doles out Rs. 2000 to an illiterate person to go and open the school and sign in the register on his behalf. Sometimes, the students get lucky and the teacher hires an educated person who also teaches them. Meanwhile, the teacher is busy conducting his own business with Rs. 16,000 that he still has. Usually, they are relatives of powerful people in the political echelons of the state.

The second most important man in the village is the patwari. There are about 12,600 villages in Punjab. Come election time, teachers and patwaris are posted on election duty. Politicians are scared of these two categories. Go on, ask me why should powerful politicians be scared of them. It is because of the simple reason that these are the two classes of people who can easily rig an election, directly or indirectly by influencing the voter. You must be wondering how can elections be rigged by these two mundane characters? Consider the following scenario.

Polling is in progress. Inside the booth are the teacher and the patwari with their teams. Illiterate voters come inside, one by one. There are new, electronic voting machines. Even urban voters do not really know how to use them. So he comes and asks the patwari; everyone know him.

"Patwari ji , kee karna hai? Machine kiddan chaldi hai?" **(how do you run the machine?).**

Patwari, if he wants to be naughty, will say *"Koi mushkil gull nahin hai! Deo, ungli phadao"* **(nothing difficult about it, just give me your finger).** He takes the man's finger and presses it on the button of the candidate the patwari wants to win. Once the button is pressed, the vote goes to him and the patwari says *"Bus! Enni gull si? Vote pai gayi"* **(this is all there to it, your vote has gone to the winner).**

The illiterate voter looks on in amazement at the machine , forgetting that he doesn't even know whom he voted for. Frankly, he doesn't even care. They have been looking after his alcohol requirements; they gave him money and probably some blankets too. Actually, both parties did that. But in the final analysis, nothing else matters to the voter. He is worried about his own survival and the next meal. His situation will remain the same, no matter who wins. His day to day life will not change and neither will his financial status. The conditions in the country will not change; the riots will go on and the bombs will keep on blasting, killing people all over the country! And he knows this reality. The politicians will be the only winners, because the looser also gains a lot, monetarily and other benefits.

The teacher works differently. Most voters have no idea what to look for in a candidate. Inside the booth, they meet an intelligent man who tells them the good points of a candidate and then goes on to explain the working of the machine. The voters are so thankful. You would be too."

"Thank God that not all teachers and patwaris are alike. May be, that is why things haven't reached the state of anarchy." said SaMule.

"Perhaps, it already is. The report published in the Tribune on 7th of October 08, says it all. From 12 to 15 per cent of class V students in Punjab could not read, could not identify numbers and could not add or multiply. They could not read a story fully in gurmukhi! If this is what is happening in Punjab in the year of our Lord 2008, can you imagine what the state of our rural teachers is and what the state of affairs would be in other states? So can these two categories be annoyed or kept on the other side of the fence? Don't even dream of doing it."

As it is, the Punjabis were the greatest sycophants the country has produced. May be it was the continuous stream of marauders that Punjab came in contact with that taught the people of the state to be on the right side of who ever happened to be in power. Thank God, people like Mehmood of Ghazni and Chenghis Khan did not decide to stay on in India. Otherwise, who knows what would have happened. We might have been sporting chinky eyes. There is an ongoing study in Mangolia to trace the genetic code of Mongols. 70 per cent of them have the same gene as Chengez Khan and they are very proud of that fact. May be, some of us have the same genes too!The white historians called him the greatest killer of all time. So why did he leave India? When the Mughuls came and made India their home, but for the Sikh Gurus, India might have been a Muslim country. Special mention must be made of Guru Gobind Singh and Guru Teg Bahadur, who made great personal sacrifices so that India could remain secular," I said.

❏

6

The Boy Craze

While waiting for my car to be serviced, we decided to watch TV in the waiting room. Some old movie was being shown. Then came a commercial break. They showed a procession in a rural scenario and the man leading it was holding on to an infant in his hands. Then they showed milk being poured into a metallic vessel and the commentator let us know that the infant was a female and this was a ritual which was followed in ancient India and is still being followed in certain areas of the country. SaMule was totally transfixed and so was I. The man holding the infant raised her to the sky and said, *"Agla ladka hoga!!* **(The next one will be a boy!!)**" He lowered the female infant into the milk. The next scene showed the milk overflowing the edges of the vessel. I was shocked. They drowned a beautiful girl just because a female child was not welcome. I noted that there were no women in the procession. Many years ago, I had seen a movie about a village in Hawai. The newborn had a scar on it's face. A disfigured child was not acceptable to the grandmother so she waded into the sea and just drowned the child. I don't remember the gender of the child or may be the gender wasn't important to them. They just didn't want a disfigured child.

Finally, SaMule spoke, "That is the difference between you humans and us animals. We give no importance to the physical dimensions of our relatives, look at this scene. If they have to kill the poor child, why go through the whole exercise of arranging a procession, wasting so much of milk and shouting "agla ladka hoga!" How do they know that the next one will be a boy and not a girl again. The female child would have died just as well in water. They could have fed the milk to some boys instead!"

Believe me, whenever the scene comes on before the start of the serial 'Laddoo.......' on TV, I get very upset. God wanted His creations to procreate. So, he created genders. I personally feel that if the women of our world had produced eggs on their own without interference from the male, this world would have been a very peaceful place to live in. But with the introduction of the sexual act, everyone is having a good time. We have found ways to go around the main function of procreation. In a way, it is a blessing in disguise. If man had produced a child every time he had intercourse, just imagine what our population would have been!

In monarchies all over the world, a boy was preferred to carry on the lineage. This feeling was perfectly logical in that scenario. But then Indians took it upon themselves to produce a boy every time, and if they could not because of the genetic combinations, then heaven help the lady responsible for producing a girl child. The reason for a must-have-boy situation is mainly for the extension of the family lineage and the fact that there has to be a son to carry the father on his shoulders to the cremation ground when he dies. Otherwise, the Indian soul does not reach heaven.

It is preposterous, isn't it, considering the fact that they say that only the soul goes to heaven and not the body. What goes to the cremation grounds carried by the son or sons, is just the body. The soul can't wait to get out of the body which was its' abode for donkey years. As if there would be a traffic barrier en route to heaven which would check if the body was indeed carried to the cremation grounds by sons. Otherwise is the soul sent back? I would like to tell my Indian brothers that the moment the person dies, the soul makes a quick getaway. It does not wait to see what befalls its erstwhile abode, son or no son.

The Indians took it many steps ahead and decided that girls were a curse. The biggest enemy of the girl child was the woman of the species, the mother herself because of the stigma attached to a girl child. Later on, the mother-in-law does her job pretty well. Many Indians kill the female child at birth. In case that did not happen, then she was treated as a second rate human, to be used in the kitchen and for household chores (the excuse is that she would go to her new home armed with the knowledge of running a home) and any other job that the mother could think of. This is not the case in all families. There are intelligent Indians who treat their daughters like their sons, or better still as one of their children, with love and affection. When the time comes for their marriage, they are married off in style.

There was a corollary to this happy ending. She could go a family which would treat her equally well, or she could end up at the end of a torch, very dead on a pile of wood. That was the ever present suspense on the newly wed bride's head like a sword of Damocles. Nevertheless, since life has to progress, the step of marriage had to be taken. The future, they said, was dependant upon the girl's destiny.

SaMule was very confused. Thus, he asked, "Why give a son so much importance in the first place? These days with girls competing with boys in every field, are they not? Mrs Indira Gandhi was not allowed to light her father's pyre. The grandson (Sanjay), according to one newspaper report, had turned seventeen by then. He was the one who put a flame to his grandfather's pyre. Why didn't Rajiv light the fire is a mystery. May be he wasn't in the country at that point of time. How does it matter if the daughter lights her father's pyre. Recently, when a daughter finally gave flame to her father's pyre, it made headlines. The beauty of it all was that the father did not come to know of it, since he was very much dead in any case. I am sure the soul, if it has a resting place in heaven, was already ensconced in heaven with it's membership to Club Heaven with all club dues paid in advance. And, St Peter at the pearly gates of Heaven did not raise his eyebrows at all."

We have many instances where the woman is killed or divorced after being married for years because she has not given birth to a son! As if producing sons is solely dependant upon the females of the species! They have conveniently forgotten the genetic factor where the X and the Y chromosomes are supposed to lend a hand in the sex of the product.

The next issue is that of property. Girls are not supposed to receive any share of the family property in India. The excuse is that the ancestral property will get divided and will naturally go to the family into which the girl gets married. Big deal! If she has to carry it along with her as dowry or if she goes into her family a rich woman, where is the harm? But the Indian social system is warped. If the girl comes from a rich family, the in-laws want more than she has brought. She will be tortured to get more. Probably even get burnt for her efforts. That way, the in-laws get to keep what she had brought and the boy is free to marry again.

The law favors the bride very heavily. If the bride dies within seven years of her marriage, the police will arrest all and sundry from the in-laws' family and tend to throw away the key, into the deep blue sea. Not that it has stopped the bride from suffering inhuman torture. Neither are we scared of the law or society, for society does nothing to ostracize the offending family. Everyone forgets, very quickly. Even as I write, a beautiful 35-year-old teacher was burnt by her in-laws yesterday. She is fighting for her life with 20-30 per cent burns. This time the reason was insufficient dowry and the extra-marital affair of the husband.

This is the year 2008 of our Lord. In the old days, people thought that the son would look after the parents in their old age. No more. Off he goes to faraway lands, looking for greener pastures, leaving old parents behind to fend for themselves. This is the male child they have been pining for and kept trying even after collecting a brood of six girls in the bargain. Such boys turn out to be spoilt brats because of the pampering they receive at the hands of the parents and the elder siblings. No matter what the girls do for their parents or how well they do in life, the value of the son in the Indian value system remains an all time high. He need not do much to earn the accolades that he receives from parents. In fact, he is the feather in their cap; so he has to be eulogized and his actions justified.

Just three days back, one such illustrious son cut off all the fingers and the ears of his brother because of family land, for which he could show no contribution. We hear of sons killing parents for money. In recent times though, we came to know of a daughter who killed her entire family by poisoning them. By and large, daughters are often more loving than sons. But we still hanker after sons. Something has to be wrong with the system.

The legal system is lacking somewhere too. If the newly married bride is burnt, why can't the in-laws be charged with murder and convicted? The system is too lenient, hence the criminals are not scared about killing the poor bride. I remember talking to my driver in Muscat, Oman. He could count the number of criminal cases on his fingers. There were two, to be exact. One, where a foreigner had gone to the police station to complain about his bicycle being stolen. Instead of writing his complaint, the police officer in-charge consoled him and said that nothing gets stolen in Muscat. He will find his bicycle lying at home; and he did. The other one was of an Indian who had murdered another Indian and then he had run into the desert. The police followed him on a helicopter and did nothing to prevent his escape. He died in the desert, for the desert spares no one.

Why isn't there any crime in those countries? In Muscat, they cut off one or both the hands of a thief, surgically, of course! Hence no one dares to steal. They also cut off the penis of a rapist. I personally think that the Islamic law would do very well in India.

In the beginning, man could go with any women he fancied. But somewhere along the line, he developed propriety rights over a particular woman and things became ugly, hence society decided to institutionalize the sexual union between two people of the opposite sex and called it marriage. When the institution arrived in India and the act got legalized, Indians took it upon themselves to provide the maximum numbers to the world population. India became the bench-mark of the world's population along with China. The Chinese Government realized that they were sitting on a time bomb of population. They put a cap on how many children one couple could produce. That, sort of kept the population of that country under control. But nothing of that sort happened in India. **The reason was simple, Indian politicians need a vote bank; China doesn't!**

We call India a secular country. In essence this means that under one garb or the other, people are free to carry on doing whatever they want to. But mostly, religion and politics are the umbrella under which everything is covered. If you are a Muslim, you can marry many times and produce as many kids as you want and can. If you are a Hindu and would like to have two wives, you can easily convert into the Muslim faith on paper and get married again. Then, the children get legal status and so does the wife. The supreme court has put a dampener on this habit. But, we have loop holes every where and one can get away from a stint in prison and is richer by a wife and many children. I am not sure if I like it personally, as an idea worth considering.

In urban situations, these days, it is difficult to rear more tham two children. Living costs have gone up stupendously. Education costs have touched the sky. No longer is it an easy task for anyone to get the child enrolled in a school. These days the schools ask for a donation, which could be any amount, catering to the flights of fancy of the authorities. The demands from children in cities is so high that most newly weds have decided against children. What about the propagation of your family name? Who cares, they say. Children are the bond between husband and wife. So, who cares? The mantra of today is — if my partner feels that he or she cannot stay with me anymore, he or she is free to go. At least there won't be children to sour up our lives!

SaMule was quick to latch on to that. He said, "Spoken like a true donkey! I love this new generation of humans. I feel they are reaching our level rapidly.

We don't have to marry. We are not overly keen to have children. We don't cater to their demands for long. If the child does come, it is a commodity belonging to the community. My master will be happy, for he gets another donkey to serve him. And, it has nothing to do with me."

But the scene in the villages is totally different. Earlier on, I had shown how our brethren from the states of UP, Bihar and Madhya Pradesh and southern states, have decided to make Chandigarh and Punjab their home. They don't have any qualms about children because, for them, every child is a self-sustaining commodity — a gift from God — and it also provides earning for the family. Education is no problem because everyone is illiterate. They have discovered that education doesn't pay in the long run.

One community is against family planning because of reasons best known to them. The ones, who come to our shores, are mostly artisans and they too do not care much for education. The end result is that these two segments multiply like rabbits. Every time they have sex, you can expect a child to follow. Thank God. they have limited sex with their own partner for they are perpetually pregnant. The others, they dare not impregnate.

❑

7

Our Sports

"Till a few years ago, India was the leader in world hockey. Now we don't exist in that sport. We had our billiards champions year after year and still do. The great thing was that it wasn't one man who kept winning. We have had so many of them who won world championships in that sport. The latest was Mr Advani. We have had our own Mr Milkha Singh who would have won our only track Olympic medal had he not committed the blunder of looking back to see who was behind him. But he came fourth. Cricket has been here and there. Apart from a few people like Gavaskar and Tendulkar, who have excelled individually, it is only now that India is really doing well in cricket. PT Usha won laurels at the Common Wealth and Asian levels in athletics. Vishwanath Anand has been at the top of the table of the chess board for many years now. Recently Abhinav Bindra won us a gold medal in shooting at the Beijing Olympics. It is our first individual medal in 108 years. Strange as it may seem, in a country, with a population in billions, we can count all our top sportsmen on the tips of our fingers. Why is that?" I wondered aloud. Then, I continued, "Just look at the games of cricket and hockey. Once upon a time the entire country came to a standstill when the Indian team played a match of hockey! When we were in medical school, the greatest sporting event was a hockey match between India and Pakistan. The whole lot of us used to gather in the canteen around the radio to listen to the commentary by the famous Hindi commentator Jasdev Singh. There was no TV then. We used to listen to each word that he would say. We used to dance like frenzied children when we won and there were people who cried when we lost. Yes! We did take our hockey seriously."

"Then other nations decided to play better than what we were playing and today, India does not even figure in the Olympic line-up, both in our men and women teams, which is such a shame. That is a big slide for a game which was touted as **the national game.** But then came the game of cricket which took away five days from the work force of the nation. Do you realize how much that is in terms of man-hours?" Neelam asked.

"No. I suppose it should run into millions of hours." I made a guess and said.

"Yes! It is much more than millions of hours actually. It was a game designed by the British so that they could enjoy the fruit of their plunder from India and Africa while they relaxed. But, wonder of wonders! We proved again that we were still as stupid as we were in the game of Tambola. Till then, Indians never challenged anyone or any concept and definitely not our slavery. But in the case of cricket, we developed this missing trait very quickly. We took up the game as a challenge, forgetting that the game was basically a humiliation for the Indian masses. While we worked and slogged for the British, they played cricket, always with a festive spirit. We had our own brown sahibs, those who could speak the Queen's language and play the Queen's game, all the while aping mannerisms of the sahibs! While they played cricket and mingled with their rulers, the rest of India watched and forgot that India was still a slave to the British. And then, many years later, Bollywood made a movie called *Lagaan*. For those three hours, we see ourselves humiliated, insulted and beaten. The movie pounds you into dirt, filth and hunger in which the villagers live in contrast to the British sahibs. They all lived in glory, ate the best food and imbibed scotch brought from England. They were served by Indian servants, who were only too eager to please them finally, the director decided that we must win the game and bring back some of our glory, through the game of cricket."

"The game of cricket serves at least one purpose. For five days, the country is re-united. Caste and creed are forgotten. There is not one instance where there was communal rioting during a cricket match," I said.

"Yes, there was no rioting on communal lines but we would break the stadium and torch it, if we thought that an Indian player had been given out wrongly, as suggested by the commentator. The ruling party was happy because no one in the country raised any issue worth raising. Before anyone realized, it was time for the next series. 2-3 months would pass off peacefully and then it was time for the Indian team to set off for a jaunt overseas for an international tournament. The whole nation forgot it's hunger pangs, lack of shelter during the monsoons and the subsequent floods and finally, the winters. No one remembered the fact that there wasn't any electricity for three days in a row and that there were areas in the country where there was no tap water. It had to be brought in containers from miles. They were so hooked on to cricket that nothing else mattered. Wasn't the Indian team playing in Australia where it was summer? They could see them sweating on T.V.

In India, food on the table is secondary. A T.V. set has priority over food. Pepsi Cola drummed up an earth-shattering advertisement which made India and the Indians realize that it is only through cricket that we will become world leaders. Hence the freezing winter in India did not matter. Politicians were the happiest. India was busy. Did the Pepsi advertisement not promise that they would also get the damsel if they watched cricket and drank Pepsi? Multi National Companies continued to rake in their millions and so did the actors who endorsed the products with cricket at the fringe. If the team did well, the Prime Minister, President and all ministers who mattered could not gather enough words of praise and if the team faired badly, the same people asked for some heads on the block."

I asked SaMule what he thought about cricket.

"I have been listening to what Neelam is saying. Humans are funny people. They are never satisfied with what they have. You are God's chosen ones. I don't think any of you would realize that. You have a brain that works differently. You have a body that is made in such a way that you can take part in these sports activities. Look at me. You think I can play cricket or hockey. Why I can't even walk the way you do? I am not complaining. But look at the way you behave. When interest seems to be flagging, a rumor of match-fixing originates somewhere in South Africa and at its root, there is an Indian. Suddenly, all those cricket lovers are shattered when they realize that the frantic nailbiting and sleepless nights were in vain.

They realize that the end result was all planned and known to the players. They made their money and you lost your sleep along with your nails, which you bit to nothingness! Then there is anger all over. People stop watching cricket. They feel cheated. Then they forget and forgive cricket's travesties, for there are new heroes on the horizon who have to be eulogized!"

I asked Neelam about her reaction to the match fixing. She agrees with SaMule. She said, "We saw our hero howling like a baby on BBC after he was charged with match fixing by an administrator who has probably never held a bat in his hands. Our hero could have asked the cameras to stop rolling till he got a hold on himself. He could have requested the BBC to censor all the flooding that took place in the studios because of his tears. But while the howling by our hero so mesmerized the country, India became the world's laughing stock. But we Indians forgot the main issue. Was he involved in the rigging stuff or not? Anyway, the issue got washed away in the flood of his tears. They did find some scapegoats and they were rightly or wrongly, crucified according to the laws of the land of scapegoats."

" Or scapedonkeys! I am happy that no donkey was involved!"

Neelam continued," The world over, violent games are played by men, which happily include boxing and the modern-day WWF wrestling. Ice hockey is a game where players traditionally beat each other to pulp with their hockey sticks and fists. The great footballer Zidane head-butted the other guy in the chest in a world cup football match. Nothing happened. He was still welcomed to France as a hero. And he wasn't even a real Frenchman. Here in India, if Harbhajan Singh, the off-spinner, gives back an Aussie some of his own medicine or if he slaps a youngster for reasons known best to the two of them, he gets hung, while the other fellow howls like a baby and the country howls with him.

"Indians howl a lot these days. Is there any special reason? Participants in reality shows huddle and howl if one of them gets kicked out, all the while rejoicing inside. When some one wins the Indian Idol show, he howls. Is the next step Hara Kiri?" SaMule asked sarcastically.

❑

8

Moral and Social Values

In the old times, India was proud of its moral and social values, for they were at a peak then. The respect for the elders was some-thing to be proud of. As a matter of fact, respect for each other was the hallmark of Indian society. It did not matter if the elder was a relative or not. It was immaterial who the elder was or if he had performed deeds of valor, or if he was dumb and illiterate. The young touched his feet and gave him as much respect as they could. He did not say that the elder had to 'earn' his respect. The elders, in turn, gave them their blessings. Teachers received that respect in abundance. The traditional double handed greeting was a must. The guest was like a God. The guest also behaved in a manner which behooved the respect accorded to him. Women, out of modesty, covered their chest with a cloth called a chunni. With passage of time, all that has disappeared.

I was asked the definition of success by Sanjiv Dutta, a very intelligent young man, "Does success mean the amount of money a person has earned?"

I said, "To a large extent, yes. One is known by his materialistic possessions, the level that he has reached in his field of work. That is the visible yardstick. What is not visible are his moral values, his achievements, other than what money can buy, the values that he has imbibed in his children, their education, their moral values, etc. In my book, those are the real yard-sticks for success."

Character of an individual has no importance. Materialism has raised its head to sinister levels. What matters is the material worth of the person. How the money was earned is of no consequence either. Modesty in the modern younger generation does not exist. The chunni, which was the hallmark of modesty among women, has almost disappeared. It has been replaced by a defiant exposure of their assets. If you have it, flaunt it, said a young girl. Parents are to be blamed for this change in attitude.

No longer do we see people greeting each other traditionally. Only the politicians use it to beg for votes. The young shake hands aping the West. A tradition which is extremely unhygienic, I am sure you would agree. With the ever increasing physical intimacy amongst the young, shaking hands becomes very handy for the next step.

The tradition of touching the feet of elders is now just a token bending of the back and an extension of the favored arm. The elders too, are not used to this act anymore. The moment someone tries to show any intention of indulging in the feet touching business, they immediately go into the reverse mode, muttering, "No, no! Please don't," instead of blessing the other party, as was the tradition. May be, they no longer consider themselves fit material to bless anyone. anymore, or old enough?! My ten-year-old grandson attempted to touch the feet of a retired Major General. His attempt was pre-empted in true army traditions and then advised not to touch anyone's feet in the future. I could see the confused look on my grandson's face because we had taught him otherwise. No wonder, the General's children think on those lines.

The youth of today are also different. They ape western society in such a way that they make certain that they are way ahead of them at the end of it all. The only difference is that they pick up the habit 20 years after the West is in the process of abandoning it. Thus the sexual explosion, drugs, crime and general behavioral abnormalities are increasing in India. The current fad of the true Christian is catching up in the West, where the youth is into virginity. It follows the rule of "no smoking and no drinking." Of course, they have their old-fashioned youth who still dabble in everything possible. When movies came into existence in India, the theme of love was omnipotent in them. But then, as time progressed, the love that was portrayed in the old movies began to take on a very unhealthy western slant.

Mrs. Reshma Harbax Singh had come to my book café to look at my collection and we started talking. In the course of our conversation, she said something worth mulling over. She felt that **the West loves but with an expiry date on it. The Indians love and carry on the pretension of love long after it is over.** I really don't have any idea if this was her original thought but I asked her if I could quote her. She happily agreed.

John Denver wrote and sang the most beautiful love song, called "Annie's Song,." for his wife. It was the ultimate love song in my book. They divorced two years later. Where did the love go? Maybe the expiry date was too short! The Indians love and carry on the pretension of love, she said. They have to, don't they? In the Indian scenario, the words **divorce** or **talaq** have no equivalent words in Hindi! So they had to stay together.

Strange as it may seem to you, divorce in the Indian system was never an option. Love had nothing to with the institution of marriage. It was an arrangement. The two were wedded and an alliance formed between two families and the husband and wife. Now, they could procreate, build a family, look after it, nurture it and let it grow. Love, if it had to come, came in due course of time. And it did; most of the time, that is. But if there was no love between the two, they stayed together despite the lack of it, tolerating each other, for their primary aim was their family. They had got together for that purpose to begin with. The husband and wife looked after each other. It was the real case of "till death do us part." In addition, the lady, in the rural setting, does it because being illiterate, she would have nowhere else to go if she lets go of her man. She would have no home or family. The man carries on because he has a comfortable arrangement.

But now, with a large percentage of women becoming literate in English, they have added another word to their dictionary: **divorce**. They decide to opt out of the relationship sooner than later. **They have run out of patience and respect for each other**. We can argue the pros and cons of a divorce till the cows come home and leave for office the next day. But as far as I remember, the vows say "In happiness and sorrow, in disease and in health and till death do us part!" I don't remember anyone saying "Only for convenience will we be together!"

SaMule said, "Thank Lord for we have no proprietary ownership rights over each otherl no weddings and thus, no divorce!"

Social values were always a mixed basket in India, as it was in other countries. We had all sorts of custom. Some of them were way ahead of the West. Like the ones in the North Eastern states and Himachal Pradesh. While I was in a Oman, the Lebanese camp superintendent told me a story about Sudan. He had gone to meet his friend for a week. They have a funny custom where the host presents his young daughter to the guest as a guide and for the sexual aspects too. This Lebanese person said that he had a great time there and even his impotence disappeared transiently.

In the north-eastern states, the women are more promiscous than men and the custom is somewhat similar to the one in Sudan. In the interior of Himachal, the Rati riwaz meant that the women of a village were available to a visitor from another village and vice versa. That is why there was a high percentage of cases of veneral disease. I am not sure if the custom exists or has been given up. There was a custom similar to this one in the state of Haryana, although it was limited to the village men folk only. If this system is still prevalent is a mystery. In Punjab, when the eldest brother married, the lady would be available to other brothers as well. The problem arose when the youngest brother would be 23 years old and the elder brother's wife was in her fifties. I had a patient in the psychiatry department where the youngest brother was a victim of this custom. He was really suffering. The children, he said, belonged to the family. This was done so that the small land holdings would not be broken up between the brothers if they all married and then went on to have their own children. In other families, if one brother died, his wife would be married off to the younger unmarried brother for the same reason. It was called *Chaddar Pauna*. I am sure some of these customs must still be in vogue. In other parts of Punjab and

India, the elder brother's wife is given the status and respect equivalent to a mother.

These days, with the newer generations going in for a single child, these problems will not arise. Uncles and aunts, brothers and sisters and cousins would hardly pose any problems for they would soon be extinct species like the dinosaurs. As it is, only a few families that still have brothers and sisters are on talking terms with one another because of property issues and other financial disputes.

❑

9

We Give Ourselves Certificates of High Moral Character Too Easily

India has the dubious distinction of supplying 40 per cent of the world's fake medicines. That is definitely a tough figure to achieve by any standards. We need to forget about the figures for the time being. Let us talk about the reasons and the end result of these deeds. One does not have to be a genius to find out the reason for doing this. It is pure and simple greed for quick money. Thankfully, the manufacturers of these medicines are not doctors. It isn't that these are men of deficient intelligence or that these people are not aware of the seriousness of the offence. They must be aware that this is an offence which comes under the category of rarest of the rare crimes.

How can any one even think that he has the right to withdraw the right to live, from a person who is struggling for life in any case? How can anyone make a fool of humanity in such a profane manner? The right to live should be withdrawn from such people. Period. Because they make, not one person suffer, but innumerable people suffer for no fault of theirs. This, after paying for the spurious drugs. If Indians supply 40

% of the "world's" fake medicines, I shudder to think what the figure would be in our own country. Yesterday, the 14th day of April 2010, a homeopathic doctor was found to be making Dexamethasone eye drops and vials of a very important antibiotic in his house! Heaven help those who have already used his products.

In an interview on BBC, it was shocking to hear a seemingly illiterate woman from Amritsar. When asked which medicines she could supply, she promptly replied "Any medicine that you need!"

People dabbling in this trade are not alone. There has to be a partnership, a nexus, between law enforcers, people who distribute these medicines knowingly and the people who sell these drugs to victims after getting them on huge rebates. How can the conscience of so many people be compromised by the common factor of greed? Obviously, only those people who have compromised themselves and sold their souls to the devil for a pittance, will join this disgraceful racket. But I am sure there must be people who are upright and have the power to put an end to this. So, why don't they? We have heard of the old saying 'If you are not against it, you are with it.'

Medical services in the country are awe inspiring. Ours is such a huge country. The standard of our doctors is excellent. Government medical services are available almost everywhere. There could be places which are very remote and health services are not exactly at the doorsteps. Accessible villages have adequate basic health services. It is a completely different story in the cities of India. Our services could be better than any place in the world. Despite all this, we have our share of scams which are frightening.

Take the case of the wonderful miracle that has saved thousands of lives and gives a chance to live better lives, angioplasty. Doctors are supposed to dispose syringes and needles after a single use. The needle hasn't even entered the blood stream yet. But catheters used for cardiac angiography, which come into direct contact with arterial blood, are used and reused! This could well be the norm in many countries. But I am interested only in India. For India is my country and I am an Indian who is worried about other Indians. These are state-of-the-art, five-star corporate commercial hospitals. I had a feud with one of the top hospitals of the region on this issue only because I had inside information that catheters were being used six times!

It is re-used as recommended by the manufacturers, they said! What they fail to tell us is that in the USA, there are private agencies which operate under the guidelines of the FDA. They are the accredited members of the Joint Commision International which oversees the recycling of catheters. These companies are equipped with the state-of-the-art equipment to sterilize catheters and the Octupus, which is the beating heart stabilizer. They are under instructions to repeat the recycling for six times.

Unfortunately, in India, we don't have the sophisticated equipment to do what they do in the USA. So some of them are known to wash the catheters and reuse the equipment up to 10 times! I have no idea why the Americans started this trend in the first place. The bacterial counts are so high that if people knew about this, they would probably decide against surgery.

As luck would have it, I had to go to the same hospital for my own angioplasty and I was petrified about the number of times the catheter I was getting had been recycled. I was reassured that it was new! My good friend, Dr. Sudhir Saxena who was the interventionist, opened new catheters for me. How many people get infected with AIDS through this route is anyone's guess. The patient is tested for HIV before the surgery and never after they leave the hospital. They should be testing the patient after the incubation period to see if the patient has been given any return gift by the procedure, transfusion and the surgery. As to the stent put in, a lot depends upon the honesty quotient of the hospital and the doctors. The difference in prices is so huge that only God can stay away from that kind of money.

I am not saying that doctors are guilty themselves. Some of the hospitals force these doctors to produce 'results' and justify the salary given to them. And please don't forget the medical companies which give incentives to doctors to use their product (read stents, catheters, titanium screws and plates). Who would not like to attend a conference in Istanbul or Prague?

Recently, an Indian doctor running a chain of reputed nursing homes in the USA, was asked to surrender his license because he was reported for reusing ordinary syringes! One was shocked! How much would a syringe cost in the US? The patient is being charged for it in any case. Perhaps, this doctor was dealing in numbers. He was using ten thousand syringes a month in his chain of nursing homes, so it becomes very lucrative. And this is probably just the tip of the iceberg! If morals are compromised in one area, chances are that they are compromised in other areas as well. That is our problem.

Please don't get me wrong. It is not that people of other countries are not corrupt. It is only a matter of degree (or difference). We are way ahead. But the old vernacular saying, *"pappi pait key leye,"* some doctors with fluctuating scruples also start to look around. Their eyes settle on the human body and the parts that it has because that is the only thing they have any contact with. Everything has some sale value. Hence the kidney scam, blood scam, cardiac catheter scam, titanium screw scam etc. Not too many doctors are involved in these but the ones who are, have definitely succeeded in throwing the light on the profession.

"Doc, there is another aspect of your profession, which in my humble opinion is most strange. Remember, it is just an opinion of a donkey who has traveled. I don't think any other civilized country would allow this sort of a thing. When your young doctors come out of medical school or get specialization, quite a few of them want to start their private practices, which is fine. It is their choice. But when the ophthalmologist decides to get some experience in cataract surgery by holding camps in villages, I think that is mighty unfair! Poor and illiterate villagers flock to these camps in the hope of getting back their vision free of charge. The camps are make-shift operation theaters where the conditions are totally unhygienic. The poor villagers have no idea what they are heading for. The cataract surgeries are done without follow up. Many old people become blind but no one comes to know. It was recently highlighted when eight or nine people became blind in a government hospital in Delhi! How can your authorities allow such a thing to be carried out? Thank God the donkeys of this world don't have to go to such people for problems of the eye.

Look at medical camps that are held by organizations like the Rotary and other do-gooders. It is a one-day affair without any follow up. If people are checked up and told about any malady that is discovered as a result thereof, it helps. The chronic cases are given a few tablets after which the patient forgets all about it since the doctor is never going to be seen again! What is the use then? There are so many people coming in to these free camps that it is humanly impossible for the doctor to sit and give a full consultation to each patient. So, what is the ultimate good deed here? The organization gets its pat; organizers get theirs. There is some satisfaction for doctors but it is mostly fatigue and patients have their one- day outing and probably, supplies of free medicines, which is neither here nor there. "

I concurred with SaMule, "I agree. I have been a part of many such medical camps and let me tell you that they were totally useless for us and patients. It is for the image of the organizers who are mainly interested in their photographs in the papers and the promotion-oriented articles about the camp. I agree with you about the legitimacy of the eye camps. They are unethical and should be banned. No other country will allow it except Pakistan, because we are basically the same."

❑

10

Adulteration

I am sure other countries have their share of wrong doers, but they would be totally zapped by the food adulteration bit. I am sure they would have gone bald scratching their heads, wondering why should any one mix water into milk, or kerosene into petrol or cow dung into condiments. Why? What is the need?

I remember that in Nigeria, one always used to be wary of the scotch bought from people selling it along the highway. A new person to Nigeria would not realize the risk he was putting himself and his family in by stopping and buying the stuff. Those peddlers could easily be armed highway robbers and the scotch totally spurious. But then, that was Nigeria. They had just come out of the Biafran war and were armed to the teeth. When they did not get jobs, they just dug out their weapons and took to bootlegging and armed robbery.

But in India, the ones who do these wrong things, are already loaded with cash and have no reason to dabble into petty crimes, excepting their insatiable greed. Agreed, these acts of petty theft have made some of them very rich. But don't they know that everyone knows about them and where the money is coming from? What good does this kind of money do? They play with the lives of millions of children and adults?

I often say that heaven and hell are here on the earth. They will get their punishment here, on the earth. The point is how many people will suffer before they receive their due punishment?

SaMule had been quiet for a while. Then he said "It is said that every one has to pay for their deeds when they die. I beg to differ. I haven't seen heaven or hell. You people insist that animals don't have souls. That is why you address animals as "it" and yourselves him or her. Heaven and hell belong to only you. But I tend to agree with you that heaven and hell are on earth itself and you do not have to die to be able to see them. Most people pay for their deeds during their life-times. The only thing is that they don't see it happening, even as it is happening. They pay for it here in the form of a disfigured or a diseased child or some other manner which they haven't connected to their deeds. That is their hell. And it is here that they will suffer. Why can't you see it? And you said that you people are so religious and God fearing. If you really were, you would never resort to these things.

"Our Yajnas hopefully look after us. We believe in and observe the navratras and the shradhs very seriously. People will refrain from eating and drinking during this period. They can have only special kinds of food. They will refrain from buying or selling or starting a new venture during Shradhs. By reducing their food and alcohol intake, they reduce their weight. I haven't seen too many people reducing though.

The younger lot has very little to do with this period of the Hindu calendar. Do the crooks also give themselves a break. Do the people who adulterate milk, petrol, condiments, ghee etc take a sabbatical? If that be so, I would recommend that shradhs be undertaken thrice a year."

Contamination continues in anything that the human mind can imagine. It is obvious that the Indian mind is the most fertile of them all. Indians use the maximum number of condiments, pepper and grams. Imagine buying edible stuff for which you have paid genuine money but get that stuff adulterated with the most vulgar and nauseating things like cow dung.

Hold on. Not everyone should be cribbing here. We have people who believe that the urine and faeces of the cow are sacred. Hence they should not crib about their condiments. Every edible thing, from oils to grams, milk to sweet meats, ice cream to ghee, honey to soft drinks, chocolate to tea leaves, coffee powder to milk powder, everything is adulterated. Even the water melon that you so lovingly have, is injected with Oxytocin, sugar and color! Why are we like this? Why do we do these things! When everyone is ready to pay higher prices which, in turn, increases the profit margin of seller, why should the greed be to such degrading levels? Why?

I will tell you why. You go to the market to buy watermelons. The first silly question that you ask the hawker is " Is it sweet and red?"

Now, the hawker hasn't tasted it and neither does he have X ray vision. But to sell the fruit, he has to say " Eat and see. It is very sweet and very red!"

Your next answer is, "I will buy it only if it is sweet and red." So, he makes certain that they are all sweet and red and ready for sale, by putting in sweeteners and color. Then, you see the sting operation on TV where they show the guy injecting color and sweeteners into the melons which leaves you shell-shocked. Didn't you wonder how the seller was so sure of the sweetness and redness? And did you imagine him to be Houdini that he could tell you the shade of red correctly or was he expected to have X-Ray vision which penetrated the melon?

Hold on! I was totally wrong about the stage where the water-melons were injected. I had surmised that the selling point was where the adulteration took place till I saw another TV expose.' When the water-melons, *kakris, kaddoos* and *laukis* were still attached to the vine, the farmer starts injecting a drug called Oxytocin into the vegetable. The water-melon and other stuff enumerated here become 2-3 times the size within 24 hours! Only in case of water-melons, there is the next step of injecting color and sweeteners. So that the seller can confidently sell his melons while you get red and sweet watermelons as your heart had desired. The funny thing is that Oxytocin is a drug injected into cows and buffaloes so that the farmer may get a larger yield of milk. Obviously, it has side effects. But then, who cares in India?

There was a TV sting operation in one of the bigger hospitals in Hyderabad. I saw it myself and it shocked the daylights out of my mind. The operation was carried out in the morgue area. And we thought that our organs went to the pyre with us. No! In that hospital, they didn't. The morgue in-charge cut out organs of cadavers according to the demand of the buyers. Each organ was priced differently. The demand for kidneys was the highest. One would again infer that it was for use in another body as a transplant. But then, liver and heart are definitely not used for transplant by ignorant buyers. And definitely not to be carried away in polythene bags! These buyers did not come in Mercedes or BMWs. They wore ordinary clothes, came walking, very much empty handed and departed walking, carrying the polythene bag with the organ of their choice. The cost was in the range of Rs 650 (liver and kidney) to Rs 1500 for the heart! No organ for transplantation came that cheap! If you ask me, it had to be for cannibalization. And we called Idi Amin a cannibal! If the person was having a heart party, he had to be partly well off, because he preferred the human heart to a turkey or chicken, which are cheaper and better to taste, I am sure.

When I saw the footage, I was shocked. Most people would be. The next episode wasn't aired. May be, it was not aired because of the gory nature of the footage. Or may be, it was, and I missed it. But I thought about it and reached a conclusion that maybe a tantrik was involved who wanted to cure a disease through ingestion of human meat. But either there were too many tantriks or the tantrik had too many clients! India has a fairly large number of them. They have incited parents to kill their own children and other people's children so that they may use the blood and intestines for whatever ends they may have in mind. I came across stories of this kind in Nigeria where we were warned to keep children within sight and indoors during election time. Certain people would kidnap small children and use their intestines for medicines to be used to make sure that candidates were victorious. I have no idea if this was true but we made sure that our children did not play anywhere unattended. But India leads the pack in the number of people who have been pulled into the racket or the number of the practitioners of tantra. Why hasn't time and education changed the way we think. They used to burn women in Europe on the suspicion of their being witches but no longer. We still do.

One goes to the gas station with absolute reverence and folded hands and a prayer on the lips. No, gas stations have not been dubbed religious places by the government. The carburetor gets choked after getting spurious stuff. There is the damage to engine. One is praying to the God of petrol that the car stays functional. And that happens almost on a weekly basis. Is getting rich so important? This is a silently proclaimed truth about our petrol outlets. There are very few petrol stations which can swear about the 100 per cent or even 70 per cent purity of their product. With oil prices touching $120 a barrel and rising, I fear that adulteration of petrol will increase.

My car, a Ford Ikon, started stuttering as if it had developed the dreaded disease of stammering. I got all the spark plugs wires changed when changing of the plugs did not help. The stammering remained undiagnosed. A mechanic hesitantly asked me to get petrol from the government-owned petrol pumps in Sector 9 or Sector 33. The very first fill cured my car by 90 per cent of its' disease. The next one cured it fully. Now, my Ford can communicate with me with ease and the drive is so much more comfortable and peaceful!

The racket of adulteration can never survive if it does not have official blessing. The fake milk that is being produced with complete impunity in so many places in the country is being manufactured after the criminals have been found out and arrested on a previous occasion. The same people start the same business again. Recently, in Punjab, a factory making spurious milk was unearthed. Nearly 25,000 littres of spurious milk were found in their possession. When I talk about spurious milk, I mean that the end product has nothing to do with milk. It only looks like milk because it is white in color and is in a liquid form. It did not have any ingredients to suggest that the liquid was a remote relative of milk. Doesn't anyone realize the monstrosity of the crime? Small children, pregnant mothers, growing sportsmen and people from all walks of life will suffer from the ill effects of this due to one corrupt man's greed. Why wasn't the perpetrator given a summary trial and shot or hanged? Why do we release these heinous criminals to get back and injure society again and again? Is it just because there are people in the administration who have been greased?

Why? If a man hacks three people in a fit of rage, he is hanged by the judiciary. If a man kills hundreds of people by slow poisoning, is the crime less? Why isn't he hung till death? The milk, if you can call it that, was thrown over the hill side ceremoniously, with the minister of health over-looking "Operation Disposal." It was splashed all over TV but what was done to the perpetrators of the crime is a mystery to all. They should have been on TV with a noose around their necks! They put blotting paper into ice-cream so that they could increase the quantity and improve the consistency.

In China, a factory producing fake milk was unearthed. They were mixing a substance called Melamine. Since then, all the milk supplied by them has been called back and two of their head honchos were awarded death sentence.

Why can't we do that in India. Why are they let off to carry on whatever they do with impunity?

❑

11

Some Idiosyncracies

Just take the mundane issue of spitting. We are a nation of dedicated spitters. We spit at everything and everywhere. Our brethren who devour the thing called paan are experts in belching out the red liquid which seems to magically spew forth in rivulets from their mouth. This habit of spitting has been conveeted into an art form. They can spit it to distances unheard of by novice spitters. These people could easily compete in the Guiness Book of Records. Hence roads, walls, buses and even clothes of passers by will be graced by the evidence of the paan that has been chewed. Why do we do that? After being called educated for years, why can't we act as educated and civilized people? Why? The sophisticated chewers of paan like the nawabs had servants holding special containers, called spittoons, into which the nawab and the likes of him would spit out the liquid remnant. But then the habit of the paan infiltrated into the general masses which did not have the sophistication of the royals and neither did they have servants holding the spittoons. So they just let it go. Where it landed was not their concern. They were just keen about the sound it produced and the distance it travelled.

Have you noticed a very queer habit, which I believe is again restricted to many Indians. When they urinate, they automatically let loose of a large blob of spit. I have no idea if women also do it but I am sure about the male of the species. Here, the technique is different. They don't let it go as they do in the case of the paan. They drop it at the place where they are supposed to donate their urine. Paan has no role to play here. I asked a few people why they do that. They were acutely embarrassed. It was as if a child was caught stealing a toffee! They fumbled for an answer and finally came out with a baffling "because everyone does it."

Yes, that is a valid reason. "Is'nt it?"

My friend, Sam Panwar, narrated a nugget from the Japanese culture A Japanese visiting the toilet on an airline will make sure that he leaves the toilet as clean as he found it, or cleaner, which means that it shall be absolutely clean. They will make sure that the basins are dry and the seat is clean before they leave, whereas, Indians will never do that. We do not do that at home. Are we crazy to clean it after we have used a public toilet on an airplane? Isn't it simple logic? Haven't we paid for the plane ticket? Why doesn't the airline hire janitors? Why should they expect us to clean the ruddy things ourselves?

"Sir ji," said SaMule, "you have missed the point here. The airline does not expect you to clean up after you have done what you were there for. It is the Japanese culture which forces the Japanese people to do what they do. Thank God! Indian influence has not reached there yet!"

There is a Chinese saying, "If every one keeps street in front of house clean, whole street stay clean."

Yes, we might agree to believe in that too. If we do clean the street in front of our house, as intelligent Indians, we will dump our garbage in front of the house next to our neighbors' house. Where else can you dump your garbage? That is what the owner of that house will do. So one fine day, the street will be as obnoxiously dirty as it was before. May be, dirtier then before!

Everyone knows that we are the cleanest people on the face of the earth. We must bathe ourselves everyday. The French, they say, are not very fond of bathing. May be, the weather is not conducive to daily bathing. May be, they are too busy doing other important things of life. May be, they have some sort of water shortage. I could not find out the reason because the French did not give me a visa to visit France. Whatever be the reason, it certainly made them contribute heartily to the world of exotic perfumery. It is different in India. Even if we don't get a square meal every day, bath is something we cannot miss. While we were in medical school in Shimla, my friend would go down to the grounds in winters, fill up a bucket with snow and then proceed to melt it with a heating rod immersed into it. The end result was a mug of water. He would then repeat the process. This was because of the unfortunate natural phenomenon of the water freezing in the water pipes in the peak of winters. Then, he would go ahead and have his blessed bath.

SaMule observed with a smile on his lips, "I have seen farmers, who were also my bosses, bathing in rainwater collected in ditches. The water was so muddy that I could not see how they were bathing themselves. Were they really bathing or giving themselves a mud bath? After that, they went on to vigorously scrub themselves clean and dry! With that, their hygienic and spiritual duty was over and they were ready to face whatever the world was going to throw at them during the course of the day (can't be anything filthier). This is exactly what we donkeys do, in the exotic company of buffaloes. Our reason is different. We do not have access to tap water. In the peak of summers, we go looking for such water reservoirs where we can cool ourselves. But imagine you humans doing that! It is preposterous. Most of you associate bathing with religion and spirituality."

"You are right. We are very religious and God-fearing as the peoples."

" Doctor! I am surprised when you say that you people are very God-fearing. Had you said that you are very superstitious, I would have agreed. God fearing people do not commit atrocities as you all do. You do have to answer to your God, you know. This is what you said. I have noticed some very peculiar traits in some of you. There are these people who wear a thread around their necks which hangs like a sash of some kind. So, every time they go to the loo, they take it out and hook it around their ears. What purpose does it serve?"

"Yes, it is called Janeyu. It is worn by the people who used to call themselves the superior castes or the Brahmins. I have no idea what a thread around the ear has to do with passing urine. May be, it is some yoga asana analogue which creates a current of some kind for better clearance of toxins from the body. I did ask some people who wore it and they told me about the five knots on the Janeyu which reminds the wearer of stuff that he should not do. But with time, the knots and their meaning is all but forgotten. Some did not know and others did not care. It was something that they had to wear so they wore it. End of argument!" Guru Nanak, being a Hindu refused to wear it!

"Quite of few of you wear many rings on your fingers. I notice you are flaunting a couple of them too."

I looked at my hand. I had two of them. One was a yellow sapphire and the other was a green sapphire. I held out my hand towards him so that he could see them properly. In fact, I was quite proud of them.

SaMule squinted at my rings and said, "Impressive! What are they for, may I ask?"

"Sure! The yellow sapphire was for the betterment of my fortune and so was the green one. The green sapphire, according to my numerologist, is a must for people with the number 8."

" So have they helped?"

"I don't know. The only thing that has happened is that the zeros have increased. So, my expenditures have gone up by leaps and bounds and I can't to catch up with them."

"So, why are you wearing them ?"

I wasn't sure if I was supposed to give him an honest answer to this. After all, this was very personal. But we were discussing personal things.

"I am not sure what they were meant to accomplish. But I was also afraid that some thing bad might happen if I took them off. Moreover, I had begun to like them. I had to take them off while playing golf because they interfered in my inter-locking grip. If I missed a crucial putt — I would blame the absence of the rings for that. This was in the beginning; now, it doesn't matter. If you miss a putt, it is too bad. The rings go back on the respective fingers after the round, taking up their ornamental role."

Samule looked at me with a smile, so typical of donkeys, and said, "Indians are superstitious by nature. You run to these Godmen astrologers, numerologists, face readers, tantriks and others for every little thing that happens or doesn't happen to you. You want money, promotion, a boy child, or if you want to remove the black magic spell supposedly cast on you by a close relative, you run to meet these people. By and large, most people go to them for money. If you look towards the West, there are more multi millionaires in the USA than all the millionaires of the world put together. But do they have the concept of a tantrik or a numerologist or an astrologer? Do they wear rings — one for each finger and one for each problem? The American millionaire has to increase his holding, not just to hold on to what he already has. Why can't we realize that these numerologists and astrologers have no role in anybody's life?"

"I think the rings help him hold on to whatever he has, what else?"

"Being a rich man has nothing to do with superstitions. Or for that matter, being a poor man has nothing to do with the movements of planets. So then, why are Indians so keen to them? The Marwadi millionaire will not leave home without consulting his personal astrologer. Come off it! This man is already a millionaire. What more can the astrologer do for him? He couldn't even make himself a lakhpati. Before the marwadi millionaire leaves his house for work, a servant or someone from the family will offer him a glass of water at the main door of his house. But a Punjabi will never have water before leaving for work. If he has to drink water before leaving, someone in the household will give him something sweet to eat before he leaves! I would say, that the former ritual works better because the marwadis are richer than the Punjabis!"

"The Marwadis are richer because they don't show off like the Punjabis. A Marwadi tends to live within his means whereas Punjabi will always spend more than he earns due to his lavish lifestyle, clubs, golf, drinking and flashy cars and many more things that he can't actually afford to get! Superstitions are so deeply embedded in the Indian psyche that it will be a Herculean task to take these out of our lives. It is not just superstitions about rings but also the remedies for many ills that are suggested by these clever people. Give black gram to the poor, throw maize chapattis to black ravens, throw five kilograms of iron into a running river, don't cut your nails at night, don't wash your hair on a Thursday etc.

But what the three highly educated brothers did to their mother was too much even from Indian standards. They beat their mother with iron rods because they suspected that an evil spirit had possessed her. When she died, they killed their sister and sister-in-law too. The brother-in-law managed to escape. This was not in a remote jungle but in the heart of Gurgaon, next to the national capital of India! Illiteracy had nothing to do with it. The brothers were educated; one was an MBA, the second one was working in an MNC, and the third one was a businessman! So, that throws the theory that illiteracy is the root cause of all ills straight out of the window.

Illiteracy is a big factor in our daily life, even if it is not in relation to superstitions. There is a very serious attempt on the part of administration to be helpful to commuters by putting traffic signboards all over. They are used for pointing out the correct way for their benefit. The problem is that in India, political parties and religious organizations have their own agendas. What better manner than to put up their posters on these boards that the administration has put up? These people think that these boards were put up for their benefit! Forgotten are the signs painted on the boards, conveniently hidden from view under these posters. **The educated students do the same during their college or university elections. They can read. But do they care? Why are we like this?**

The Indians take pride (thank God, we still have some pride left) in being the most religious and God-fearing people in the world. We have so many personal and public gods that it is not funny. There is a very poetic overtone in the whole statement. Who is religious? The one who goes to the temple very frequently or daily or has God in his heart, even if he doesn't go to pray in the temple, gurudwara, church or mosque? Are the visit or occasional thoughts about God more important or in the God-fearing deed more important? In India, I am afraid, telling the whole world about how religious you are is more important than your act. Hence, you have to tolerate the bombardment over loudspeakers, destroying the happiness of all and sundry and the processions blocking roads and causing great inconvenience to the common man at large.

In foreign countries like the UK and the USA, people are very religious too. But nowhere, will noise filter out and disturb the general public. I will not comment about Muslim countries for they have their own system. In the USA and Africa, people from African backgrounds have different churches where the devout sing the verses very loudly. This is accompanied by dancing but no one else is disturbed.

It is only in the Indian subcontinent where we carry our religion on our sleeves and our religious places are used as centers of noise pollution for the non-believers or people who believe in other faiths. If only we could make religion a very personal thing and not something that you have to flaunt on the street, I am sure riots because of religion would be lesser. I did not say that rioting would cease, for in India, religion is used for their personal agenda by political parties and rioting is a very potent weapon. Hence they can never end. More over, do we have only one reason for indulging in this national past time of rioting?

Noise pollution that is being produced by the zealous faithful goes un-noticed by the perpetrators. They don't know how much harm is caused to the hapless students preparing for examinations. They are probably sending a very religious message to students to have more faith in God than in themselves, for divine intervention will help them more in exams than the cog slips that they so seriously manufacture.

In the villages of Punjab, gurudwaras are the main source of religious proclamations. As a matter of policy, all of them broadcast religious hymns from loudspeakers the whole day long. When asked about the reason, their reply was that it is for the benefit of the whole village and it is nice to have religious thoughts during the day. They forget that the village population has people belonging to other faiths as well, who have no interest in Sikh scriptures or the scripture of any other faith. But who cares? Must we be like this?

If religion is so important to us, why can't we acknowledge that religion is equally important to the other man too? And if we can't respect the other man's religion, we don't' have the right to kill him for his beliefs. But Indians do that all the time. We take out our anger on the people of the other faiths. We burn them as well as their places of worship. We wipe out all traces of it, as they did in the recent Gujarat riots. Why are we like this?

We go to the other extreme. Indians in southern India will convert ordinary film stars into gods, make temples for them and worship them. These are gods who are common to all communities. May be, it is better this way. At least there is no acrimony between communities and there is no incident rioting, raping and burning.

In places which are dominated by Muslims, the maulavis read the Quran over loudspeakers in their typical intonation. The Hindus have their own share of jagrans which carry on through the night using the dreaded loudspeakers at full blast. They too think that they are fulfilling a social obligation to the whole community and to those who could not attend the jagran for some odd reason. May be, it has not occurred to them that the ones, who did not turn up for the jagran, did not want to attend. I pity the family which stays next door to the Jagran and who might also be non believers! The only choice he is left with is to attend the function and stay awake while accumulating points of good inter-religious behavior with the neighbor.

"I remember that many years ago I was invited by a friend to his Jagran function. Not realizing the importance, a friend and I had already taken a few pegs of whiskey. As we entered the venue, my friend came over and said, "Mataji gets these powers some time during the proceedings as she goes into a trance. She will ask the people who have had liquor to leave or else face the consequences." My friend and I exchanged glances and decided to leave and let the lady do what she was there to do.

SaMule laughed, "and in the bargain, you got a chance to slip out and have a few more, eh?"

They are not aware that noise is also pollution which contributes towards the kitty of oxygen-free radicals responsible for 95 per cent of diseases which afflict the human body. The argument that they would put forth is that the common man is hardly bothered about noise pollution. Look at the noise levels in weddings and music being played by the huge stereos people have in their cars. The counter argument would be that the noise from religion is on a perpetual basis. If it is not one, then it is the other. I asked my friend, Sa Mule, about the jagrans and loudspeakers in the places of worship.

He said, "You have me here. We are totally guilty. Donkeys bray without much provocation due to some reason. I must add here that the decibels during my own braying are sometimes uncomfortable for my ears as well. But I cannot do much about it because God has provided us with this apparatus without volume control. But still, our braying is not half as much irritating to the humans as is the artificial noise which emanates from your loudspeakers and horns."

"Ha!" I said and added, "That is what you think. Your braying is something no one can withstand. It is senseless and it is the only thing I can't really stand about you and yours! Imagine a donkey standing in the middle of nowhere and braying without reason and without any end in sight!"

"Point taken but you have occasion galore. Parties, religious, political, electoral, pre and post spiritual gatherings by a deluge of Gurus that you humans have. In smaller cities I have noticed the advertisement by theatres proclaiming the screening of a new film. Oh! The list goes on and on. Why is it necessary for you to make so much noise. In the West, such things are not heard of. The noise pollution by honking on the roads is absent. In the African sub continent, they can not do without music since it is in their genes. And one should not forget the dancing."

"Yes. I once saw a young boy in Illorin in Nigeria, with stuff in both hands and a tray laden with eggs, cigarettes and kola nuts balanced on the head, wanting to cross the highway. Mind you, the highway in those countries is not like the ones you see here. People drive at speeds of over 120 kms on an average. He crossed but danced all the way to the sounds of music emanating from a roadside pub! I was totally zapped!"

The horn is very important in the Indian traffic scenario. Smaller traffic on the road presents additional hazards to themselves and to the other heavier vehicles, hence the need of perpetual honking. So how does one manage to control the traffic and limit speed? When the Czechoslovakian badminton team came to Chandigarh, they were amused by the amount of honking that was going on the roads. In comparison to other Indian cities, Chandigarh is mute. An amused member of the team said that it was music to his ears because in his country they never get to hear a car blowing it's horn!

❑

12

Caste System

The caste system, which was supposed to have been banned in the country has happily come back with astounding vengeance. Actually, it never went away. You just can't wish such a thing away. For hundreds of years, Indians ostracized their fellow Indians for the caste system that they themselves created. People of a lower caste were not allowed to cross the road when an upper-caste Brahmin would be walking down that road. They were not allowed to go to the same temples. They could not draw water from the same well. Their children could not play with the upper-caste children; neither could they play on the same playground. But they were allowed to die for them. They were definitely in the army which fought to save their skins. The blood that gushed out of the wounds of the lower-caste Indians was the same as that of the brahmins. What I do not understand is what took them so long to realize that they were being persecuted. Why wasn't there a revolution, as there was in France? Were they actually no better than animals in mental terms?

Many hundred years ago, Guru Nanak Dev ji had removed the caste system from society. Or at least, he tried. Then, during Guru Gobind Singh's time, four out of the five Piaras (the chosen ones) belonged to the so-called lower castes. When it was the time for langar (community food), people from all castes sat and ate together. This tradition is still followed in the Sikh religion.

Could only Mr. Ambedkar come and tell them what to do? And today, when they are of almost equal status in most of India, why do they want to go back proudly to be called STs and SCs? Why? Isn't it a victory for them when the so called upper-caste clamors to be one of them? They should be satisfied with that and then decide to join the mainstream, trying to build a strong India. No, that is not happening. The population of OBCs has risen by 5 per cent!

It is more than 60 years that India won the so called 'Independence'. People, no matter what their social or financial status, clamor to be labeled schedule castes or tribes or as they popularly are known as, OBCs. In the state of Punjab, where the Jats consider themselves above everyone else and next to only God, wanted to be included in that list, irrespective of who they were or what their land and financial holdings were. It is such a marvelous gesture in magnanimity. I agree they get percentages for jobs and seats in professional colleges, amongst other things. But only an Indian can do this. What is the value of such pride? Zilch. Zero. India is the only country which still has this disgusting division between humans in this age, when other people are thinking about more important things.

I admire these people so much for their humility and zeal with which they want to downgrade themselves; to bring themselves at par with the other classes of the country and happily rule over them through political means because of the wealth they have accumulated over the years. Well, you can't have everything! But sincerely speaking, owning big areas of land, having multiple houses, children getting the best of education in India and abroad, living like kings with swanky cars, having the latest gadgets at your disposal and finally, be able to criticise the country and everyone else over a bottles of liquor in the evening as a part of your social obligation. What else can a man hope for? Only the right to be called an OBC is left — so that they can get the few things which are left over for the common man? Humility always pays in the long run!

Only in India is this category of the OBC prevalent. In the recent riots, by the Meenas which caused so much hardship for everyone, the reason for the riots was not religion or politics. It was the right to be called an OBC! Why are we like this? An OBC will then loose the right to visit a temple graced by an upper-caste Brahmin! He doesn't mind that. He can always build another temple for OBC's and ban the Brahmins from entering the temple. In any case, very few people seriously go to the temple for the sake of offering prayer.

SaMule said "See, humans have always been selfish. They will try to get some leeway from anywhere. A system which caused them so much hardship in terms of pride, lost chances in education and in life generally, will be embraced again because of the freebees, like getting a huge percentage in interviews for jobs, seats in professional colleges, the administrative services, promotions etc. They have forgotten the fact that they had been ostracized by one and all. Now they have a chance to undo all the wrongs; but they want to settle down in the quagmire of reservation and go back another 300 years. Why don't they study, which a lot of them are doing? They should be working at par level. Instead, they are looking for freebees; any kind of dole that they can wrangle out of the government, without actually deserving it. I am not competent to discuss your issue of religion, although simple logic would force me to say that if one is part of a religion, piece-meal acceptance of its tenets is not good. We don't have a concept of religion but if we had, then I would honor it in it's entirety; specially, when one is never welcome in another religion. On the face of it, yes. But deep inside, there are a lot of reservations. The Pakistanis call the Muslims who migrated from India after partition, 'mujahirs' and they are not respected at all. Then there were non muslims who were allowed to stay on in Pakistan after they had renounced their faith and embraced the Muslim faith. They were never accepted as an original muslim and were always looked down upon. Why would they accept a convert?"

The right Honorable HRD minister of India had mooted the concept of 27 per cent reservation in the seats of medical colleges, engineering colleges, the IIMs etc. for the OBCs. It was vehemently objected to by the children of non-OBC and non-SC and non-ST parents. That just meant that people with lower marks but armed with their certificates would get preference over brighter students. In April 2008, the Supreme Court ruled in favor of the OBCs and their brethren.

This has happened almost 60 years after India has gained her 'freedom' from the British! All this, while the OBC's have had the right to best of education and the best of administrative and professional jobs. My heart bleeds for those children who have worked so hard, got unbelievably wonderful marks and still face the uncertainty in getting a seat in a professional college or a job, all because their parents were not farsighted enough to get them an OBC certificate; all because of the politicians who feel that the initial period of ten years wasn't enough for them. Hence, they gave them ten more and then, 10 more and then 10 more. Finally, after 60-odd years, they get their reservation. Never mind the quality of doctors and engineers and management graduates that India will be flooded with.

In the state of Punjab, they are so liberal that it is not funny. I talked about the video screening in the villages of UP. There, they are told about these foolish Punjabis who will feed them, wash their utensils and some idiot will also be polishing their shoes in the gurudwara. I did not believe it. I thought these people only came here for work. One trip down to the Golden Temple in Amritsar cleared all my cobwebs. As the time for the langar (community food) to be served approached, there was a stampede of sorts. I quickly jumped to one side because there was a chance that I would get trampled upon. I asked someone what was happening.

He said,"this is a daily occurrence. Women, children and men will leave their work and run with their utensils so that they can eat to their heart's content and carry langar for the night so that they do not have to come here again."

With eyes wide open in disbelief, I asked him, 'Can't you do anything to stop them?"

"Sardar Sahib, you have missed the entire philosophy of Sikhism. This is the Guru's langar. No one can be turned back hungry. With the grace of the Guru, our langar has never fallen short. So let them bring the whole of the states of UP and Bihar. We are ready to feed them!"

At a later visit to Gurdwara Dukhniwaran Sahib in Patiala, similar scenes were witnessed. They were sitting next to devout Sikhs and not one of them objected to the filthy lice-laden humans sitting next to them. They had brought their tiffins for the evening meals with them. Our visitors ate as much as they could, the Sikhs serving them exhorted them to have more. Ultimately, they got their dinner packed, left their plates where they were, to be picked up by the sevadars and washed by another set of sevadars. Those who had brought along their foot wear, found them to have been cleaned. They happily left with bright hopes of returning the next day.

When hurricane Katrina destroyed New Orleans and people were starving, there was one community (the Shiks) of 'do gooders', who did not just collect money for them. The ones who owned hotels, opened their doors to whoever cared to stay with them, free of charge. The ones who did not own hotels, carried truck-loads of food packets under the garb of langar. And they did it not for the Indians but for the inhabitants of the country which had opened its doors for them and anyone else who cared to partake the food brought by them.

It is a different matter that once their crisis was over, the Americans forgot what the Sikhs and Punjabis had done for them and what they even looked like. They killed a few saying that they were the Taliban, Iraqis or whatever they could call them, thus displaying their lack of intelligence. Can this noble act be replicated by the visitors from other states to Punjab? I doubt it. Because you have to have the heart of a true Punjabi! One has to be ready to sacrifice. Only a Punjabi can sacrifice his own food for the unknown. They feed thousands upon thousands in the free langars in gurudwaras of the state of Punjab and elsewhere, day in and day out.

"That much is true," said SaMule.

Religion and the caste system has other complicated ramifications in the south of India. The devdasis were young girls who were taken up by the temples for the service in the temples as dancers amongst other things. They were also used as prostitutes without being given that title. That practice is still prevalent in India. There are temples in the south where only a certain class of people may visit to offer their prayers. Recently, in Gujarat, a temple had to be washed and purified because a low- caste minister had gone there to offer his obeisance. In the villages of Punjab also, despite their generosity and big heart, there are separate gurudwaras for jats and tarkhans. Even in foreign lands, one finds this segregation of Indian places of worship very prevalent and extremely distasteful. One wonders, why are we like this? Sikhs I said were so magnanimous but when it came to their own religion, there is such a huge dichotomy of thought and they become so petty, forgetting the basics of what Guru Nanak had taught them. Why?

The London constabulary was baffled by this behavior of the Sikhs. The Sikhs routinely attacked each other with swords and kirpans. So, the Superintendent of Police posted a constable in one of the major gurdwaras of London. His job was to study the erratic behavior and find out the reason for it. After a month, the constable put in his report.

His report said, "They are a bunch of very religious people. They come into the gurudwara, take off their shoes as a mark of respect. The ones who do not sport a turban, cover their head with a large cloth provided by the authorities. I too have a readymade turban which I wear on entering the gurudwara after removing my helmet. They bow their heads in front of the holy book and settle down to listen to holy hyms sung by their singers in utter humility, moving to and fro in rhythm with the music. I must add here that the hymns are very pleasing to the ears. After the singing is over, the congregation stands for the prayers, called Ardas. They again sit down to receive the brown pudding which they call Parshad. It is then that all mayhem is let loose. Turbans go flying, swords are out and if I may add here, Sir, it is very dangerous. All said and done, they are nice people!"

Why do we do this? We are a bunch of God-fearing people and our Gurus have repeatedly taught us that the ego should be banished. So, why can't we do that and stop making fools of ourselves? Fighting over what, may I ask? Control over God's house? Or, is it just control over the finances of God's houses? Or, is it just a matter of control? Ego of a few people, who probably know more of the Lord's scripture theoretically!

But I also met a very different kind of a person very recently. He is called Akaliji and is an Ayurvedic doctor. I heard about him from a patient of mine. His friend had been diagnosed as a case of chronic renal failure and he was practically on his death-bed. On a strong recommendation from some one, they came to Akaliji and told him the symptoms. A medication was prepared and sent by courier. Wonders of wonders, the patient became mobile and till the day of this writing, I was told that the patient is improving. He also told me that he treats hypertension and in just eight days, there is no sign of it.

I got very excited since I have been hypertensive for the last 30 years. I wanted to take that chance. So, I went along with my wife to a village on the outskirts of Patiala in Punjab. It was a typical village scene. It was dirty as hell. There was stagnant water everywhere. There were carts full of expensive and exotic fruits. I commented to my friend about the presence of abundant expensive exotic fruits in a scenario like the one we were passing through. Could the villagers really afford them?

He said, "If these people come everyday to sell their produce, someone is buying them!"

Finally, we came to the residence of Akaliji. There were a couple of diwans placed in a haphazard formation. A couple of sofas also adorned the remaining space. People were sitting facing all directions. No one seemed to mind if someone had his back to him. In one corner, sat a very young, good looking lady with large jars separating her from her patients. She was Akaliji's daughter, a graduate in Ayurvedic medicine. She was unfazed by the crowd and went about her business of asking symptoms, dispensing medicines from her cupboard and the bottles in front of her. She was also in charge of collecting the money. I think that she was also very aware of her own good looks in a scenario of that kind.

Soon, we were introduced to a frail man in his early sixties. He was told that I am an allopathic doctor from the PGI and wanted his medicine. He almost ignored that bit of information. Any other man would have gloated over the fact that a senior doctor from another mainstream of medicine had come all the way from Chandigarh to take his medicine. He did nothing of the sort. He made us sit down and proceeded on a discourse of the relevance of the the Granth Sahib

(Holy Book) in relation to the body in health, sickness and disease. He quoted extensively from the Granth Sahib and all the while, I was thinking about the middle that I will write in The Tribune about him, Shri Guru Granth Sahib Ji, the clinic and the kind of treatment that he gave to patients.

I took his medicine, touched his feet for no specific reason, received his blessings and left. It is a different matter that in eight days, from four tablets, I was down to one. Since I am such a chronic case, I thought I should be taking his medicine for some more time. But I stopped his medicine after some time because of the bitterness of the preparation.

❑

13

The Almighty Currency

Talking about politics, there is a symbiotic relationship between politics and money. They attract each other like honey attracts dust. Money is definitely involved in politics both ways. If you have money, you want to join politics or you want to hobnob with politicians. Either way, more money comes into play; but then money is involved in everything all over the world. It is money that makes the mare go as they say. Our sages have also called money currency as in electric current. It should remain into circulation. Otherwise there is darkness. It is also like blood circulation. Stasis results in thrombosis.

Since politics is such a high tension area, a lot of this currency automatically circulates towards politicians. They are very conscious of their duties so they keep it into circulation, lest there be embolism. They build huge mansions for themselves, buy the best of cars. Their children study in the best schools of the world and their holdings cross the seven seas.

They are not the only ones though. Children of the elite services class are supposed to have been born with lead coated golden spoons in their mouths. They cannot send their children to study abroad with the kind of salaries they give themselves. The perks will not help.

But they all end up going anyway. We have discussed this in some length earlier.

SaMule was in deep thought. And then very pensively said," Doctor, why are most of you so obsessed with money?"

"Spoken like a true donkey. Come on! Can you do anything without money? The food that your master gives you is bought with money and soon, he will let you loose to graze on your own because he won't be able to afford what he gives you. That is why we are obsessed about money. Everyone has to feed his family. In order to put food on the table and look after the needs of his family, he has to have money!"

"What I meant was that no one wants to work for what he was hired. He begins to look for ways and means to make that extra buck. He doesn't mind the fact that he might be stealing it from his place of work or getting it illegally. Why is that so? Where is his pride, his self respect?"

"Because he can't make two ends meet. Because he can't buy the things that his family wants with what he gets. He loses all self-respect and pride when he cannot be the provider. Once he starts dabbling into dirty money and becomes the provider for his family, his family begins to look up to him. Thus, he regains his self respect, despite the fact that he can't look at himself in the mirror on most mornings. "

"Are you blaming the family for his ill-gotten gains?"

"In a way, yes!"

"Did he not start to work in that organization after he agreed to the terms and conditions? He agreed to work for that pay package? So, once he gets the job, he suddenly feels that the pay is not enough and he should steal from the company. A policeman should start work only when he gets his cut? What would happen if the army did the same. What would happen if doctors would start looking after patients only when they think that they have made sufficient money? What if all teachers start taking tuitions instead of teaching in schools and colleges that they work in?"

"I will tell you something that my mother told me very recently. Did I tell you that my mother taught Mathematics, Hindi and Punjabi in a public school? No? Well, she did. She had four friends who were also teachers in the same school. They were all wives of very senior IAS officers of the Haryana and Punjab cadres. In 1964 till the early seventies, the ladies received a mind-boggling salary of Rs two hundred and fifty! My mother and her friends had a sari kitty out of their salaries and were thrilled when they got their sari, which must be worth something very nominal. That just shows you how honest their husbands were. Had they been corrupt, would have they let their wives scrounge for a sari? I knew them personally and I am proud to have been associated with them. One of them is still around and he has been playing golf every day, pulling his own golf cart! I am sure being the Chief Secretary of Haryana would have given him sufficient loopholes to make that extra buck, but he did not. That is how some people earn their respect. "

This cannot be said for every one though. Problems arise when people from other professions realize that they too are short of the almighty currency. Some of them, like doctors, are better qualified than most Indians. Why, they wonder, are they still the lowest on salaries and perks; they get the most useless houses compared to their administrative service counterparts. So, they start looking around for a reason and they find out that they are labeled "honorable profession members" along with teachers. They are expected to be 'honorable', meaning thereby that they are not supposed to be rich themselves; and people belonging to other professions are not honorable. Thus, they can collect as much currency as they want.

Teachers are by and large very honorable. They have been doing their duty impeccably. The students look up to them as role models, their heroes. Still, there are those few who realize that they too need money so that they can live comfortably and send their children to good schools and abroad, if possible. So they call their wards for extra tuitions. All said and done, they are not harming students; they still teach them and bring them up to the required standards.

We have teachers who have been indulging in student bashing. Some poor children have lost their hearing, some their vision and still others, their lives. Why these teachers cause physical harm to the poor students is a mystery. They also indulge in sexual aberrations where they forcibly involve their male and female students. Does this happen only in India? I am sure it happens in other countries too, but we are concerned with the happenings in India.

We have been fed with stories about the great traditions of the teacher-and-student relationship prevalent in India for centuries. The teacher was held in greater esteem than God, for it was the teacher who educated us about God. There is a story about the great teacher, Dhronacharya, who is the archery teacher for Arjuna and his cousins. Dhronacharya took sides and played favorites. He liked Arjuna more than the rest of them; that too despite knowing that Eklavya was a better marksman than Arjuna. As the story goes, Dhronacharya schemed to make Eklavya look inferior to Arjuna, asked him for a kind of fee, called gurudakshina, a fee that the pupil gives to his Guru, his teacher. But he did not ask for a materialistic fee. He asked Eklavya to present him with his right thumb, which was most important part in the art of archery. Despite knowing this fact, Eklavya, without any hesitation, cut off his thumb and presented it to his teacher. Now, Dhronacharya was satisfied that there could be no better archer than Arjuna.

But look at the devotion of Eklavya. Such dedication to a teacher is not a common thing; in fact, it is unheard of. This was India for many centuries. Even today, teachers in India get a lot of respect; but not from every student. I remember my teachers very well. Forty years after leaving my medical school, I have enough respect for my teachers that I have no hesitation in touching their feet when I meet them. Has this changed? My mother and wife are on the receiving end of this adulation from people who were their students 25 to 50 years ago. Dhronacharya was a mortal with defects in his psyche. Was it really justified to respect him to the degree that Eklavya did, knowing what he had asked for was wrong? Not many students in any era would have agreed to his demand. It was Eklavya's greatness as a student. That is why he is remembered even today. Whereas, most students today would have asked Dhronacharya to climb the nearest tree! But Dhronacharya, being the teacher of teachers that he was, thumb notwithstanding, is respected to this day and a National award has been instituted in his name for sporting Gurus, celebrating their talent as Gurus in their respective sport.

I think that perhaps an award "Eklavya Award" should be instituted in the memory of Eklavya, so that modern day students can get fired up and become ideal students in the true tradition of the past.

What is the status of education today? I asked SaMule. His answer was typical.

"Don't even look at education in my circle. Keeping in mind the job that we do and will most probably carry on doing, education for us is redundant. If after being educated, humans still steal, kill, rape and do all kinds of things an educated person should not do, then I can safely say that it was better when you were uneducated. All of a sudden, my self worth has gone up by leaps and bounds. I feel very superior to humans.

As you know, I move around a lot. Generally, in India, the standard of your education is good; at least in some pockets of the country and in certain segments of your society. But in India, there are so many children who have not seen the inside of a school. Why is that? Poverty is the foremost reason why parents are not in a position to send their children to school. They would rather have them earn their share and help in bringing food on the table. That is one reason why the lower class produces so many children despite the fact that there is never enough food to feed them all."

In urban situations, a Right To Education bill has been launched, where schools, private and government alike, have been asked to accommodate some percentage of the below poverty line (or the BPL as they are referred to), students into their schools. It is a beginning but the bill has been at the receiving end of bouquets and bricks alike. It will take a long time to change the thinking of children and their parents, where the importance of education over earning, will have to be explained. The other factor of hygiene is equally important because these children from the slums give very little yardage to hygiene. A large percentage of them suffer from lice, scabies, tuberculosis and other infectious diseases. If they have to mingle with children of the upper strata, education in this aspect will be very important. The concept of uniforms in these people is non-existent. There is another aspect of the mingling of the two strata. These children who were being asked to work in homes as help or in shops and were contributing to the family kitty, suddenly realize the change in their lives and their thinking pattern changes. They will be reluctant to work as helpers in households and will end up demanding various things from their parents and soon the parents will resent that attitude. In short, these children will be misfits. The government should set up separate schools for them and not distort their thinking by mingling with a class of people they are not a part of. I am not against the RTE but at the way they plan to run it. The attempt must be at teaching them vocations, where they will learn trades and then go on to earn a livelihood and be useful to society. Just by studying till class 4,5 or 8 will take them nowhere. This partial education just goes to their heads and they think that they are ready to receive the goodies that life has to offer them, something that society is duty bound to give them just because they have gone to school.

"But it is already too late. You 'won' your independence from the British more than 60 years ago. What were you waiting for? When you insist that you won your independence, you almost compare yourselves with us. The only thing is that we haven't seen any other life. We would not know what Independence is and what to do with it. But you all knew what independence was before you let it be taken away. And you stayed like donkeys for more than 200 years. It must have been interesting. Pity! I wasn't there," said and SaMule snorted again. I really hated that snort. But he was right.

SaMule has been around the country. He said, "In cities like Chandigarh, Delhi, Mumbai and a host of others which boast of Golf clubs, we see hundreds of children from under-privileged families earn a decent living as caddies. They earn between 70 to 100 Rupees per round. And chances are that on some days, they may get to caddy two rounds. If a child or a young adult can earn and contribute money to the family kitty and he doesn't complain, why should any person raise an issue which doesn't affect him at all? As if this person had ever done any thing good for these children! At least by being caddies, these children are around respectable people, learn to speak a lot of words of another language, learn to behave, they learn to dress properly and stay off the streets; stay off begging, drugs and crime.

Many times, for good caddies, CEOs of companies have opened job opportunities. A CEO of a multi-national company, Mr Bharat Ram, had picked up a caddy, Rohtas Singh, when he was a young lad, to be his personal coach and with time he started treating him like his son. Rohtas Singh went on to be a national level professional golfer and won many laurels. If you see him now, he would easily be mistaken for anyone from a very upcoming family or even better. May be, the bidi would give him away. Hundreds of caddies have picked up the game and have become professional golfers. I have seen scores of caddies who have undergone a sea change during the time I have played my golf in Chandigarh Golf Club. I have seen them as small 10 year old children caddying for beginners like me, coaching me on shots, the mistakes that I committed during the execution of shots, my stance and my swing. The same caddies exhorted me to use the driver when I didn't have enough confidence to use it. They taught me the worst case scenario! They would say, "What is the worst that can happen if you use your driver? You will spoil a shot? So what?" I see those very caddies, twenty years later, turn into fine young golfers, working at jobs, raising their own families and generally leading crime free lives.

At one point of time, caddies constituted most of the professional golf circuit of India. The game gave them respectability and money. Rohtas Singh, Ali Sher, Ranjit Singh, Harinder Gupta, Chowrasia, Basad Ali and Akbar Ali are a few successful boys of those times. They have done so well for themselves. Ali Sher went on to win the India Open twice. If some do-gooder had put them into school and kept them away from the golf course, they would never have made two ends of their lives meet. And they would have been paupers. Quite a few of these caddies are from families which have made sure that they go to school till the 8th or the 10th class. Some have then left studies and taken up full time caddying. Yet others have taken up jobs elsewhere.

Yes! I agree with organizations which look into the vagaries of child labor. This practice generally should be abolished. It has its' inbuilt problems and will be extremely difficult to solve. The way I look at it, only 1-2 per cent of the children involved in child labor will be saved by relentless effort on the part of the NGOs. I wish them luck.

In Rio (Brazil), street children make life hell for shopkeepers. They were killed on a regular basis while they slept on the pavements by policemen hired by harassed local shopkeepers. At least our caddies are off the streets. And most importantly, they are alive!

❑

14

Idiosyncracies: Some More of Them

Ah! The mobile phone! The latest gizmo on the block! The world is after it with a vengeance. Anyone with or without the means to possess one, has to have one. Indians have started talking all the time. Some parents are happy that their introvert children are opening up. It has proven to be a boon for many professionals, specially the flesh trade. The point is that, if we can afford this small marvel, then why can't we ensure its' proper use? We go to attend meetings, to see movies, to job interviews, to see the doctor; and we conveniently forget to turn it off. These days, the master of ceremonies makes a strongly worded request at the beginning of meeting to delegates to switch off mobile phones. Still, with the seminar in progress and the speaker explaining a vital point, a couple of phones are bound to go off .

SaMule said, "The joke of the day was when the cell phone of the master of ceremonies started to ring to his acute embarrassment, minutes after he had requested the audience to switch off their mobiles! Remember the expression on his face? I couldn't help laughing. Normally, there is not the slightest embarrassment on the face of the owner while his mobile is happily and loudly singing a crazy tune or song. Glares from other members get deflected off the gentleman with élan, as if he were made of steel.

"I have been on the receiving end of the mobile many times. Imagine the scenario: The patient is supposed to switch off his mobile when he enters the doctor's chamber. He doesn't do that. On the contrary, while I am waiting, he carries on a discussion with some person, and suddenly he begins to lamblast the guy on the other side, threaten him with a lawsuit, all for my benefit. He forgets that he is not there to prove that he is superior to me. He is there for a medical consultation. The patients in the waiting room, who are ill too, are getting irritated. Does anyone care? After observing this scenario, do you suppose the people in the waiting room will switch off their sets? Your guess is as good as mine. The only place where they will switch the sets off is in airplanes, because announcements by the stewardess includes a clause which says "that it could prove a threat to life because it interferes with the electronic equipment of the plane". That really scares them.

In our Indian Medical Association (IMA) meetings, this request is standard. It should be understood that doctors too are human and have a right to show off their mobile sets and the fact that their innumerable patients call them at all hours. But it can be put on silent mode, can't it? After all, if they have become doctors, they were intelligent to begin with. Understanding this small issue should not be too difficult for them? Right? Wrong! You should hear the music emanating from mobiles in the highly academic atmosphere. Some times, the audience gets so engrossed in the lecture that they fail to realize that it is their mobile that is spitting out the loud Punjabi " aaa-ja nach leh nee" ring tone.

Etiquette also says that the mobile should be switched off in posh restaurants and clubs, where people pay good money to have a meal in peace. But then in India, can that be possible? The man could be an IAS officer, a high legal luminary or a high ranking police officer or even a minister in waiting. Can any waiter dare to ask them to do what the management desires and what the rest of the clientele have a right to? Hence, the chances are that we will be relegated to listening to all kinds of ring tones, no matter where we are. We will also be inadvertently listening to what happened in the meeting with the CM, (chief minister, if you please) or a high-sounding scheme with great flourish. Why can't we learn? No one is interested in what you do or what the CM said to you and what you said to him. I am there for the sole purpose of enjoying a good meal. Nothing is going to change in the country by your conversation. Least of all you!"

Neelam said, "Look what happened to my husband the other day. We were traveling in our car when a foolish girl driving a two wheeler, with her ear stuck to her right shoulder and a mobile phone lost somewhere in that space, oblivious of the world around her, lost control. Suddenly, a cyclist came in her way and with great difficulty, she held on to her balance and the mobile, missing us in the bargain by a whisker. My husband shouted at her to stop talking on her mobile while she was driving. She gestured rudely to my husband to move. My husband called her "bat-a-miz" and we drove off. Little did we realize that she had rung up her friends and by the time we reached the next round about, there were at least half a dozen boys armed with baseball bats. Had it not been for me and the people on the road, my husband would have had a tough time along with a few broken bones to say the least."

"You people are just paranoid. Mobile phones definitely increase the social status of an individual.

That, incidentally is the reason why people hold on to it all the time. If he possesses a top of the line cell phone, he is put on a pedestal by society. But if he is carrying 2 or 3 of them, he is almost said to have made it in life, a demi-god. The mathematics in this case is simple. He is in a situation where he can afford to buy three sets. Then he should be able to pay the rentals for them. Finally, if he is carrying three sets, he must be having three sets of ears to be able to listen to all of them together. That, my dear friend, separates the boys from the men!"

"So how does one change things around here?" asked SaMule.

"How can you change the country when you can't change a wrongly worded form used by millions of people. On record is the driving license form. It contains 4 pages. The doctor has to sign on the same wordings on both sides of pages 3 and 4, twice; and so does the poor man who is looking for a driving license. Why? If you ask the people who dish out the forms, they have no clue as to who the brain wave behind the form was. Actually, there was no brain behind it. Must have been an ass. Sorry, my friend, just a slip of the tongue. And neither is anyone interested."

I have been signing so many of these forms but since I go to the medical section only, I missed a very interesting slip, which my friend Robin Nakai pointed out to me just today when he came for his license renewal. In the check list for the residence proof , point number 'b' says, " life-insurance Policy at least 'sex' months old with latest receipt.' I had a huge laugh. I felt sad too — that a document to which the authorities give so much importance has not been studied. I think someone heard me, for that slip has been rectified!"

O.K., so it is a printer's devil. Why give it so much importance? I ask SaMule to donate a few pearls of wisdom.

"Why is the driving license so important for you? In any case, it serves no purpose. People drive without knowing any rules and frankly, no one cares. Ideally, a license is issued only after a properly conducted written, oral and driving test. Have you appeared for any one of those in India?"

"No!" I answered very honestly, "the only test that I have seen being conducted in earnest was the one they did in Nigeria!"

"See what I mean? You being educated, don't go through the motions. The influential ones get it through other means. Others buy them after bribing some official. Every one knows that the license is a fake. So why do you waste paper, manhours and energy. It would have been OK if you had been donkeys and had our patience to stand in one line for hours to get the forms,; then another for another few hours to pay the fees; then another one to deposit your form only to be told to come back after lunch to get your photograph clicked for which you have to stand in line again. Why do you people want to change a perfect human being into a donkey?"

I had no answer why we wanted to change into donkeys from the humans that we were supposed to be. I desperately wanted to change the subject.

Smoking

There has been a lobby of people who have been waging a war of sorts against smoking. They have been fighting against pollution caused by smoking and the number of people it kills. In my opinion, smokers are the most selfish people on earth. They smoke with careless abandon and utter disdain in their homes, clubs and offices, forgetting the fact that each cigarette produced three trillion oxygen free-radicals, which are responsible for 95-98 percent of the degenerative diseases known to man. The side slip has the most hydro carbons and cause innumerable hardships for those who become passive smokers for no fault of theirs. Small children, women and their unborn children suffer horrendously.

When they smoke at home, their near and dear ones come under attack. When they smoke in clubs and offices, their friends suffer. These days, young girls and their mothers smoke too. One sees children smoking.

The Chandigarh administration took great pride in announcing Chandigarh to be a green and a smoke free city. They spent a lot of money on posters which they put up all over the city, held functions where the administration patted themselves on the back and announced fines. That was the end of it all. On paper, no one was allowed to smoke in corridors, theaters, offices and public places. The airport was also included. I had gone there to see off my son when some smart looking executive types started smoking like chimneys while standing next to my wife. My wife happens to be allergic to cigarette smoke. Sensing my desire for a tête-à-tête with them, my son told me to 'chill.' But then there are some things I can't help. So I went up to them and said "Chandigarh is a green city where you can't smoke in public by law!"

The gentleman gave me a funny look as if asking "Are you for real?" He asked sarcastically, "Is that so?" Then, he carried on puffing. I looked around for a policeman but the ones hanging around were smoking too. I thought of ringing 100 for the cops but then I saw them slinking away to a corner and after a few more puffs, decided to hang up their boots, so to say. I then realized that if the administration has no will to enforce a law, they should not pass it just for the heck of getting a few pampering pats from their superiors. Chandigarh continues to be a green no smoking city and it's residents continue to puff away to glory!

As I write this, the health ministry has made smoking a crime in public places. It is an exercise in futility. We do not have enough law enforcers to curb crime. They are all busy protecting the VVIPs. How will they fine people for smoking. Yes! The smoking in public places can be curtailed by the security staff of malls, cinema houses, clubs and airports. So that much is a boon.

Other than that, I doubt if any one else will listen.

SaMule looked at me with his usual snooty expression(to which I was getting used to) and said, "If enacting a law was enough, then there would be no crime, no murders, no thefts and definitely no rapes, for there are laws against them. Why will an Indian stop smoking. Specially when he feels strongly about smoking and believes that no one has the right to tell him not to? The realization has to come from within, and for that, the general population has to sort out it's own demons. The government was making so much money from tobacco that they did not want to put an end to it. Now, all of a sudden, one minister has coined new slogans and wants to put an end to this so called 'vice'. Technically, he is right. It is just that the timing is wrong. His priorities are wrong. There is too much else happening in the country which needs attention."

Politics, Elections and Supporters

I have often wondered about the election system of our country or for that matter, any country. It goes deeper than one man or one party getting elected. What makes millions of people leave their lives behind them, go into the streets and canvas for one man or one party?

What I fail to understand is the psyche of the people who support candidates. After all, when it is all over, only the candidates and a handful of cronies will gain materialistically. Electoral gains are mostly materialistic; But what happens to the supporter? Because he rises again and again from the ashes of the previous election like a phoenix to support a new candidate, every time.

What I need to know is: if some one is so interested in elections, why not let him go on his own steam, using any means at his disposal to reach out to the masses and get elected if he is found to be fit for the job. The same can be done by political parties where their individual candidates can canvass for themselves. Solidarity is one thing. People can show their solidarity by a rally or two. But not by stopping to work for days on end. In any case, these politicians never do any work, at least not for the country. Nor do the supporters of political candidates and parties. Do they do any work for society? Yes, I do see them come out in hordes to break up theatres, coffee shops, break up the offices of newspapers or opposition parties or to throw stones at policemen.

Not that this wishful thinking will change things. I am just appalled by the selfless patience shown by Indians specially while canvassing for someone; a majority of them don't even know the man and neither have they met him. All this, despite the fact that not all politicians are above board, that they are a bit short on morals and will work for their own upliftment only and that they will not be reimbursed for their time. So, what makes them tick?

There is another set of people in the political scenario who are the backbone of violent political riots. So, they will rape, loot and kill people who they don't even know on the order of their bosses. The Indians excel in this activity due to some vague reason. I wonder if they have already chosen the woman who they will rape when the riots commence? Or, is that the woman is just unfortunate to be at the wrong place at the wrong time? Why would they gang-rape a woman? They convert the beautiful act of sex into the most barbaric animalistic performance and I am sure, they do it under the influence of liquor. The act of rape is gory and filthy and they go many steps ahead and convert it into gang rape! I shudder at the thought and pity the woman. At the same time, I thank God for not making me a female of the species.

The quantity of liquor consumed to turn them into animals has to be so much that they no longer know whether they are coming or going. In fact, they most certainly get no enjoyment in the act itself. Even their performance under the influence of alcohol is suspect. The most gruesome act is when they rape a pregnant woman and then slit open her tummy. If rape is a such a huge necessity, isn't the act enough? Must she be killed, along with her unborn child, in the most horrendous manner because she belongs to a different religion, caste or political party?

SaMule said "You said that you are lucky you are not a woman. Sir ji, being a man, they won't rape you but cut you open if you are the object of their desire on that particular day."

"I know. Haven't I seen that happen during the 1984 riots?"

"I know that you aware of all that I am saying. Have you done something about it? I just want to shake the country out of its slumber and sit up and take notice and do something. The law has not even been able to convict anyone involved in any riot. The whole idea behind the rape thing is to demoralize the men of the opposite camp. When they hear about the details of what was done to their women, they feel degraded and most demoralized. This is the *modus operandi* of any invading army in times of war.

If these criminals are paid money, it cannot last till the next riot. The TV or other household things that they plunder will not last a life-time, for there will be newer models which keep coming in the market. But the shrieks of the people they killed stay in their ears forever. Every morning, when they look at themselves in the mirror, a murderer and a rapist will stare back at them. So, why do they do it? If someone has already decided on a plan, the reason has no relevance. It can be created. The train that was burnt in Vadodra in Gujarat eight years ago, has been said to be a pre-planned attack by one community and thus, the political regime of that state stood exonerated for any excesses that might have been inflicted in the aftermath. 1180 people of a community were slaughtered in the aftermath. The 1984 riots against the Sikhs was also a pre-planned act but they said they had a reason. I feel that they would have carried it out, reason notwithstanding; even if Mrs Gandhi had not been murdered, for the powers that be, had already made lists of Sikhs in every locality of every city in the country, collected iron rods which were used to smash bones and skulls, the inflammable powder which was used to burn fellow humans and their houses, all over the country. The attacks against the so called 'converts' to Christianity are again pre-planned. The reason can be thought out later. Let the killings be done.

Have the leaders sat back and thought on the following points?

- What did they gain and what did the country lose?
- Was what they gained more than what the country lost? Was it worth the effort?

- Is it because they do not think about the country at all and are just satisfied by short lasting gains?
- Are their acts justified by their religion? Ours is a non violent religion, is it not?

Even politicians can't be that stupid. They too must be thinking because they propagate themselves as the greatest thinkers in the country as a group. But they are nearer stupidity, as we have seen time and again.

"There is a unique phenomenon in your riots. No one takes the blame for starting them but everyone takes the credit for bringing them to an end. Look at the intelligence of us animals. We might fight momentarily over a female of the species, or for our territory as in the case of dogs and the big cats, but it is all temporary. But in the case of humans, riots are terrifying. They are serious. People are out to kill each other. It is not a question of just killing but killing in the most heinous manner that can be thought out. Why do you do it?" SaMule was actually deeply hurt. He said, "No one in the country is working for the country; everyone is for themselves and every party is for itself. Once election comes to a bloody end the opposition parties make life so miserable for the ruling party that instead of dedicating it's energies towards the betterment of the country, the ruling party gets bogged down in activities which would ensure that they are still in power for five years. Hence, very little activity involving the progress of the nation is seen."

At this very moment, the health minister thinks that the idea of legalizing gays, legalizing live in relationships and smoking are more important issues than people being burnt or hacked to death. He does this so that he is always in the limelight and every issue of this kind fuels his election campaign of the future.

SaMule said, "I am not a political person. I have no interest in who wins or who sits in the presiding chair. Donkeys do not have elections and neither do they have a political party or political ambitions. We are not evolved. But in your case, the ones who get elected, spend the next five years trying to hold on to their seats. The ones who have lost, spend five years scheming and plotting ways and means to unseat the ones who are seated. In either case, there is no contribution to the welfare of the country or it's citizens. They spend crores upon crores of Rupees on these elections and then, they tax the common man till his tongue hangs out. I notice that some times, the ones who had lost the election, succeed in their nefarious designs and manage to unseat the ones in power. They have many ways to do it though. They can raise the nuclear issue, poverty issue, Ramsethu issue, Babri Masjid issue, Ram Mandir issue, and if everything else fails, organize communal riots or riots on the basis of son-of-the-soil issue as they have started in Assam now. Once they have succeeded, crores of rupees are spent again on re-election. The hyenas will have their corpses. The vicious cycle then starts all over again! It is interesting indeed!"

❑

15

We as a People

We are a funny lot. Our actions have no logic. SaMule and I had gone to the place they call God's own country, Kashmir. Indeed, Kashmir Valley is beautiful and rightfully called by names given to it by poets. But I found the people different. More than a hundred people got together and burnt a beautiful bear alive. The only misadventure the bear was guilty of was becoming hungry and straying in search of food to an area where humans ruled the roost. When it realized that it wasn't welcome, it decided to go back to the woods. But humans are unforgiving. They smashed it with stones, rods, bricks and whatever else they could lay their hands on and then set it ablaze; while it was still alive, if you please. If cruelty is so deeply embedded in our blood, what the so-called terrorists do is not very extra ordinary. They shoot people, but the victim dies an early death, unlike the one people dished out to the bear. In Canada and other parts of the world, bears have a free run and they roam across the country side too. They enter houses in search of food but no one in the world does what the Kashmiris did to the bear they caught.

On the other hand, a boy, called Prince, falls into a pit and the whole country goes stark raving mad for days spend a few lakhs or fupees. The official rupees and try to save him a few others like him. The media forgets that there are other things happening in the country too. The next footage you see is of a handsome 10 year old boy whose bicycle has been damaged by a marriage procession. He is upset and demands money for repairs. A few of the marriage party take him to a secluded place, sodomize him and then set him ablaze. Are we for real? Is this the turn of the 21st century? Come on. We did not even do this when we were in the caves, man! Now that we have come out and are called civilized, is this how we justify our ascendancy to nirvana?

TV zooms on to a group of people who have caught a 'suspected' chain snatcher. The crowd did not even find the chain on his person. The policeman ties him to his motorcycle and drags him till the poor fellow becomes unconscious! Is this how we dish out summary justice in India? If you have to show summary justice, do it for the murderers, the sex offenders, the people who adulterate milk and food stuff that we and our children consume, and our petrol and diesel. Get rid of the scum of society; the people, who organize riots and kill unsuspecting innocent people, get school children hooked on drugs! One is shocked to learn of young boys and girls in a secondary school take drugs because of drug peddlers.

Then, they shed crocodile tears over a child (Prince), who everyone had initially refused to help. When they found out that there would be TV coverage on national hook up, they readily agreed to act as saviors. And the generous corporate world donated clothes and money for the mother and invited them to Mumbai for reality shows. If they could, they would make money from corpses too.

How come we don't bother about these people? Despite the fact that we know who they are, no one wants to touch them even with a barge pole. Why?

Parminder Pal Singh Tethi is an advocate I have known for years. As I was pondering over this point, he arrived on the scene. Over coffee in my clinic, I turned the question over to him. The difference between a lawyer and a doctor is that the doctor's mind moves faster than the lawyers mind which goes into hibernation when a decision has to be made. That is why they take so long to decide. Doctors, on the other hand, have differential diagnosis to do. They do that, and then they strike at the disease with the swiftness of lightining.

He said, "It is simple. The politicians bestow their blessings on the heads of these people. That is why they canvas for politicians in elections. Short-term gains are monetary and materialistic gains; long term gains are the patronage that they enjoy. In fact the definition of a VIP should be: a person who can break the law with impunity. But the pity is that certain laws are made for the benefit of the VIP, so he need not break them. He has to break the laws meant for the common man and then get away with it. That is his claim to fame!! There are umpteen situations where the law can be broken. One does not have to be a Government servant to be a VIP. I can be a VIP if I have enough support to break the law. Look at these children of VIPs. The kids are not VIPs per se but they have the backing, hence they break all the laws the law agencies make and get away with it. They fire their revolvers in public, kill people, enter into one-sided duels, steal and manifest road rage that is enough to kill. These are the real, modern day VIPs. And we should be very wary of them." Thus, he ended with a note of caution.

Patriotism

The Indians as a people have always been very patriotic. Where the country is concerned, people of all religions rise to the occasion. For us, India has always been our mother. The best reasons behind the rekindling of the feeling of unity among the Indians were war, hockey and cricket. Hockey can safely be deleted as a valid reason. You can add festivals like Diwali and Holi to the list if you like but they too are being relegated back-seat and are no longer uniting factors.

Out of all these factors which bring out our patriotic instincts, war has been the number one. Indians go berserk while donating their money. Normally, women will part with their collection of gold and ornaments only if there is a gun on their heads., That has been our forte, our strength. But in the recent past, that strength has been eroded by the shameful acts of a few persons.

In the recent war with our neighbor, popularly known as Kargil War, despite the fact that it was our army commanders who missed the intentions. The build-up of troops and weapons by Pakistan, the people who had to fight and die for the country, were the common soldier and their young officers. So, they did their job in measures of bravery that cannot be described adequately in words. But the ones who were supposed to be plotting the tactics of war were busy making money at the expense of the soldiers dying for their country. The infamous coffin scam is so shameful that one has hardly any words to describe it.

There were two aspects to the Kargil war. On one hand, the bravery and magnanimity of Indian soldiers in general and the degeneration of the moral fiber of some of their officers on the other, because of greed in a few. On one side, the whole nation donated their money and ornaments to the war effort and on the other side greed forced other men to undo the entire good will in the country. A US firm supplied 650 aluminum caskets and 3000 body bags at a cost of $ 1.80 crore. The deal cost the Indians a whopping $ 2500 per casket and $85 for the body bag. When the same company supplied the caskets and the body bags to the UN in Somalia and the US Army at $172 and $27, respectively. Obviously there were scores of middle, men involved but the main senior officers were charged.

At least, the Americans look after their dead soldiers with respect. When Sargent Uday Taunque of the US Marines died in the Iraq war, their Generals came all the way to Chandigarh, his home town, to attend the funeral. They were here to to honor one of their dead soldiers, who belonged to Chandigarh.

It is a different matter that they don't have too many Americans who want to fight the war. Hence, they coax and bribe the Indians, Mexicans and people from other third-world countries who want to make out a living in the U.S. These persons must willing to fight and die for the US. It is, indeed, a small gesture to have a paid holiday in exotic India! But one has to pay the devil its due and applaud their behavior.

In the Bangladesh war, our senior officers had to be caught because of their corrupt behavior. They stole whatever they could lay their hands on. What would they have done? The teak certainly would have made their house look good but the money that they saved by stealing wood and taking it all the way back definitely did not make them millionaires. Even if they had become multimillionaires, getting caught and the subsequent ignominy of being cashiered cannot be traded for any amount of money in the world.

It is not that these scams are not occurring in other countries, but we are not concerned with other countries. We are just wondering why 'we' do it. Our naval secrets were passed on to the enemy. Is it justified? None of the officers were forced to do it; they did on their own free will; out of sheer greed. Do we need that? Does dirty money matter in the long run? Most recently, a staffer in the Indian High Commission in Pakistan has been caught passing on vital information to our enemy, with whom we had multiple full scale wars, daily border skirmishes, terrorist aided attacks on our soil etc. The reason for this treason was quoted as revenge for being mistreated by seniors!!! If it had been China, SaMule, do you know what the penalty would have been? But then, this is India, where we can't even execute a terrorist who was caught with all kinds of evidence and was responsible for the deaths of innocent Indians. We just don't have the guts. Iraq executed Saddam Hussein and his cronies in a short time. The amount that is being spent on him every day, could easily finance many institutions and hospitals of the country. Probably build a few vital roads or bridges in rural areas. We have a whole lot of misplaced priorities."

"Don't ask me these complicated questions. In our world there is no concept of money, dirty or otherwise. I think you should shift back to barter system. I believe, in the very beginning, it was a barter system, till currency took over. That seems to have started all the rot in your value system" SaMule answered, "Patriotism is not just about scams in the armed forces. It is about the corruption in all walks of life. It is about respect, pride and love for your country. We would not misbehave with any foreigner who comes to our country as a guest. But what do you do? Nowadays, you cheat them, fleece them, rape them and kill them. No patriot will do this. His pride for his country will not let him do these things, for the guest is like God. In the olden days you said, *Atithi Devo Bhava.* So, if you forget your old social values, patriotism would also be lost in the process. Patriotism is also about how you represent your country's values when you visit another country, for you are the country's ambassador in a small way."

❑

16

The Class System: Have We Changed at All?

India is such a vast country consisting of different religions and classes, that governing it is itself a Herculean task. There has always been a class dichotomy, which is getting into a very peculiar situation. Earlier, we had the rich and then we had the poor. The middle class was sandwiched somewhere between these two and was the pressurized lot. They could not do what the other two classes could openly do. Since all social rules were apparently created for the middle class and by the middle class itself, it remained oppressed.

"How were they oppressed?" asked SaMule, my friend.

"Simple, yet very complicated. The upper class has no taboos what so ever. Sex is open. Multiple partners are accepted in their society. I mean that there is no frowning upon by other members of their class. Drinking and smoking openly by both sexes is a done thing. The lower class does exactly the same things without any restrictions. But the middle class had to do everything in the closet. The rules that they had framed for themselves were so strict that there was no way that they could do anything openly. It was something like a professor of cardiology sitting in his office in a striped Indian underwear and a vest; and people would say, "See how humble this man is! The guy has no ego. He is a professor but see how simply he is dressed!" But if the samething is done by me or any other doctor of a lower rank, people would humiliate me and say, "He has no sense. How can a doctor sit in his office dressed like that! It is insulting to patients! This is truly shameful!"

"In other words, the middle class was dying to do all that the other classes were doing, but their rules did not let them. Who made these rules any way?"

"The middle class is the one that framed these rules. In recent times it seems that the middle class has gone overboard. See what has happened to foreign festivals like Valentine Day, Fathers Day, Mothers Day etc. These festivals are alien to us. But we have accepted them with open arms. We have not just accepted them, we have also become mad for them. We are like that. Will the Americans celebrate Onum or Diwali like we celebrate Christmas or Valentines Day? We are basically like monkeys and apes. We will ape the white man in almost everything.

The upper class is not delving exclusively in this. They might not even be celebrating any of these. It is the middle class that has taken over. There is very little difference between the upper and the middle class in the urban situation. I doubt if anyone can differentiate between the two. They wear the same clothes, drive roughly the same cars, barring a few. If just the upper class had dabbled with Valentines Day and given roses and balloons to girls, it would have been accepted very easily. But the liberated middle class is a whole new ball game. No one really remembers Saint Valentine. That is a day when you can do what you can't dream of doing on other days; that, it is alright to tease girls and vice versa; that it is alright to approach unknown members of the opposite sex and propose. Surprisingly, it is not just the boys who are a party to the whole thing. Girls belonging to the middle class are doing the same thing too."

"But your middle class has gone over board in other spheres too. Look at the music videos that are being made these days. The ones from the south of India are as obscene as the ones that are made in the North. These are totally alien to the Indian culture. But who cares. In South Korea, cable TV was banned because they felt that the cable was polluting the Korean youth. But the Government of India has no will to control obscenity, despite the fact that they have a censor board with respectable ladies on board. The problem with the boundries board is that it has become too liberal and the difference between the normal and obscene has become blurred," said SaMule.

Neelam was sitting, patiently, listening to our comments. She interjected, "There was a time when the four letter word could not be uttered in respectable gatherings. Suddenly the up coming sophisticated upper class started using it and then their children never stopped using it. Now, no one cares. The lower class was forever using that word."

"Yes! I agree with you. There was a time when we were in school. Girls used to wear skirts which were almost ankle length. If some one wore a below knee skirt and by mistake the knee showed, it was very erotic. Then, the length of the skirt grew shorter and shorter to midis and minis and now girls wear attires which are just like under wear clothing, and no one raises any eye brows. The worst part is that the woman is no longer erotic

Eroticism has successfully been removed from the female anatomy. Younger generations will grow up

looking at these images of women and think that this is the standard attire for women, whereas men have to be overdressed. May be, eroticism will have a new face and body, that of the male. Women will then be wondering about what is hidden and will swoon when a man shows his knee cap!"

"But let me tell you that this is not the face of the Indian male or female. I am aware of your heritage. Open sexuality was never a part of India. Despite the fact that Kamasutra is India's gift to the western world, it was the West that brought it out into the open. The copycats that you are, you have copied them and started behaving as if it is all new and you too should do everything openly as they do. The West has sexual orgies. It is the closest thing to the animal kingdom. Animals have sex in the open and don't mind one bit if there are spectators. The West is doing the same thing."

"Look at our own festivals and observe how they are changing. Our best known festival was Diwali. It was a festival to celebrate victory of good over evil. Ram defeated Ravana and that victory was marked by Diwali. Slowly, it changed to cleaning the house. We are busy white-washing walls, buying new utensils for the home, exchanging sweets as a token of goodwill among friends and finally, bursting crackers. It was still a simple festival with a meaning. That has all changed and it is a rat race now. One can see people running to each other's houses to drop off gifts which have been given to them by some other friends and finally you get back what you had gifted to someone!

They have forgotten the saying :

"In this rat race, even if you win, you are still a rat."

Sweets have been replaced by costly articles ranging from glass stuff to gold and diamond jewelry, depending upo whom one wants to impress and bribe. The token sweets have become *passe*. That, in a way is good. India is sitting on a Diabetic bomb. So, if they remove sweets completely, I will not complain. Again, it is the middle class which is still holding on to age-old traditions. The lower class has become so distant from these celebrations because of the price rise that I doubt if it can enjoy such festivals anymore. But I would not bet my life on it."

"Yes, yes! I really miss those sweets. I used to get a lot of the leftovers! They were just yummy. I am upset. You humans had a good thing going; why did you have to go and spoil it, is totally beyond me. Why not keep greed out of it. I have come to know that the common man takes the best of things like almonds, pistachio and kaju for your VIPs. Their rooms are stacked with goodies. The VIPs, in turn, have found a solution to the overloading. They sell them back to the dealers. This is another way of utilizing a bribe."

"So what can the VIP do with all that stuff? He can't eat all of it, you know. Their well wishers are duty bound to 'give', so they give. There has to be a gracious receiver too! The VIP can't be rude and refuse. Then there is the problem of plenty. What should they do with all those eatables? So they suggest jewellery of some sort. "

"But instead of selling gifts, why not spread them among your friends. There are other means to accept bribe. A gift should be treated as such and should not be sold. At least, this is what happens in the world of donkeys. Ah! I get it. You feel that it wasn't meant to be a gift in the first place. It was a bribe."

"We had one VIP who made it known that he was not interested in cash, hence he received superior brands of alcohol. The crates of whisky that he got were sufficient for him and his friends."

SaMule snorted. I was beginning to get bugged with his snort. Patience, man, patience. I kept whispering to myself.

"What are you whispering about?" SaMule caught on.

"OK! This is bribery and corruption. This has been a part of our culture. See what is happening to our games. In the olden times, when someone hit a six or got someone out, the spectators got up on their feet and danced according to their loyalties. These days, almost naked women dance when some one hits a four or a six, while the spectators clap at the girls, ogle at the wares that are being exhibited and pass leering comments and wonder if they are free for the evening. And then, the girls complain that "these spectators do not let us work. They add that they are not 'those' kind of girls. They also say that they dance only for the sake of spectators.

"Thank God there are no dancing donkeys in our world, otherwise a lot of sexually aroused donkeys would be running after them. But if things carry on like this, then the day is not far when this culture will pollute us too," said SaMule. Then, he added, "See, this culture of chorus girls has been imported from the USA. But when anything arrives in India, you people think that you have to 'go beyond' the originals. If you have to go down one step from next to nothing, it will be nothing. I hope that is not what you Indians have in mind? Seriously, you people are such kids. I wonder when your growing up process will begin.

First when the huge Australians used to breath down your small statured players using all kinds of expletives, your players did not retaliate for fear of being beaten up. They acted as if the sledging, as it is respectfully labeled, does not affect them. In fact, as if it fell on deaf ears. One wondered if they are actually deaf. Seeing the guy MacGrath all worked up, even donkeys would get riled. But the Indian cricketers were saints and practiced yoga and other methods of self control." He snorted again and carried on, "All of sudden one sees the new generation of cricketers who border on to belligerency. They have started giving crap for crap and sometimes go overboard, till one of them is supposed to have called an Australian a "monkey". An Indian 'brain' converted the 'monkey' to something rhyming, "teri maan ki." It is the beginning of a very degrading abuse. This was tolerated by one and all and they said "Yes, he did not call him a monkey but just abused him. An abuse is not that big a crime as being called a monkey! What crap! Just because you humans cannot tollrate being compared with your ancestors. You can happily call each other donkey and owls and no one gets wild. But call the other person a dog or a monkey and all hell breaks loose. Why is that? You don't like being reminded about your lineage. I accept that part about monkeys, but why the anger against dogs? They seem to be very near to you humans. Most of you have them as pets in your homes, something that you will never dream of doing with donkeys! It is the size thing, yes?"

"It is funny that you should bring up this subject of monkeys. I was in Nigeria in 1983, when the Nigerians were just beginning to get fed up of Asian expatriates. I was told that the Africans in general hated being called monkey. I made a mental note of that. In 1984, I decided to leave Nigeria, for the simple reason that their violence against the Indians was rising. Just the other day, they had burnt a bus with its full load of school going children. Luckily, the Nigerian driver got them all out and saved the situation. I went to Lagos in connection with my tickets. In the street, a small-sized Nigerian confronted me and gave me a long and hard stare. I did the same thing but clutched my briefcase a little tighter.

"You! Monkey!" he said.

Ahaan! I knew the trick. He wanted me to get angry and start an argument. There might be a scuffle and in that time, one of his friends would relieve me of my briefcase. I tightened my grip a little more and acted as if I did not understand what he meant by the word monkey.

"You say?" I feigned ignorance.

"You monkey!" he repeated, his voice louder this time. I could sense the tension as other Nigerians seemed to converge around us. I told my companion to stay cool and act dumb.

The mounted policeman sensed what was going to happen. He rode towards us scattering the crowd and the little one disappeared. I looked up at the policeman gratefully and made a quick getaway. My pulse took a fairly long time to settle down. Long after, I kept wondering why did he call me a monkey? He could have started the fight. But may be, he wanted to give back in the same coin and feel superior? May be, some expatriate called him a monkey and got away with it. At the end of it all, I concluded that he just wanted to create a diversion so that the group could relieve me of my belongings. So much for monkeys! That incident in Lagos still gives me creeps. What if that fellow had relieved me of my passport, tickets and money? And, if in the melee, someone could have decided to stick a knife into me? What would have happened? No money, no passport and a knife sticking into my belly in a foreign country! It would have been a bad scene."

I carried on, after a contemplatively pregnant pause, "It is said that a country is as great as it's people. I know India has the capability to be a great nation. So why are we not the greatest country? Is it because of the fact that Indians belong to so many different religions, speak so many different languages, have such diverse cultures that these factors make Indians completely indifferent to each other; bonded together only because we live within a common geographical boundary which is then called India? But! All said and done, no matter which state we belong to or which religion we subscribe to, when it comes to national issues we are all bonded together as one. So, when Major Rathore wins the silver medal in the Olympics, the whole country rejoices. Rathore becomes an Indian and is not a Rajasthani from the state of Rajasthan. The rest of the country will not let him be just a Rajasthani. He was also a member of the Indian armed forces and not just a Rajasthani. When Abhinav Bindra won the gold medal in the ten-metre shooting at the Olympics, no one in the country said that he was a Sikh belonging to the northern city of Chandigarh. The celebrations in Tamil Nadu were as great as they were in Punjab. No one said that just 24 years back, he and his relatives were thought to be responsible for the murder of Mrs. Indira Gandhi, although at that point of time, they manage to slaughter, burn, rape and kill 2600 Sikhs in the country. It might be a figure for you but just think of the logistics. Nearly 2600 wives became widows. At least a thousand children lost their fathers. Nearly 1500 parents lost their children. Finally, 2000 households were destroyed. The country lost 2600 good workers too! So why is that we, the citizens of India, forget that no matter which religion that person is from, he is basically an Indian. Why do we slaughter our own in riots that we manage to manufacture time and again?

SaMule, as if waking from his slumber, said, "It is not that this behavior is typical of Indians. I have some knowledge about human behavior in general. If you go back in time, you will realize that you have been quite heavy on the killing side. Killing animals for food and sport has always been in vogue. But humans never killed those animals which could be domesticated. Hence donkeys, horses, cats, dogs and elephants were safe from their killing habits. Birds were a mixed bunch. The ones that could be eaten were killed and the rest of them like the eagles were left free. The parrot was allowed to live because it had its' utility as a pet. Otherwise, killing has been a sport for you. There were some who were cannibals and ate each other, there were other times when watching people kill each other was a favored past time, as in the case of gladiators in Rome. That is why I call the world of humans barbaric. Today, people love watching the WWE wrestling only because they love to see men battering each other. If there is blood flowing, all the better. Can you imagine animals doing this to each other? You will argue that animals don't have evolved brains and can not think of stuff as humans do. The ones who do kill and eat other animals do so because that is their food. They don't make a spectacle out of that killing. Finished! Thank God for small mercies!"

SaMule carried on from there after a pause, "The fact that human ego is so overpowering that everyone wants to be strong and powerful; and what better way to demonstrate that power than to be proven physically superior than any other. The final proof of power was to kill your adversary and be declared the strongest. Then came the country. Each country had to show their superiority by conquering the other country. There was mass killing and plundering as an aftermath; the spoils of war, they called it. There was misery and suffering on both sides. Everyone lost a husband, a brother or a father in the wars. After the mourning, everything was forgotten and people were ready for another war, forgetting that the earlier one had not helped in any way. All countries have a history of multiple wars; of killing thousands upon thousands of people but you just never learn, do you? When it comes to civil wars, you have been at your worst. People of Croatia had cut off the limbs of their neighbors and hung them on their drawing rooms walls as souvenirs. They gouged the eyes of their erstwhile friends and offered them to their officers! These were the people with whom they had interacted with for years. They probably shared meals and drank together. So, what happened overnight that one suddenly became a Muslim and the other a Christian? Did that man sprout feathers or horns. Did he grow four arms? Did he stop defecating? Nothing changed externally. Only the thought process of people changed. One looked up to Christ and the other to Allah. They forced soldiers and citizens of the other religion under their custody to drink their own urine and eat their own excreta. All this after the concentration camp atrocities of the Nazis where they killed millions of Jews and gypsies just because they were considered to be inferior to the superior German Aryan race!"

But, the Indians consider themselves superior to everyone because of their prowess in spirituality. Just because a few of you were good in telepathy and Yoga, and that too hundreds of years ago, you consider the whole race of Indians superior? Where is the spirituality now? You people are morally degraded today. Can you imagine a country celebrating its' Independence Day? They say you have existed for 60 years as an independent country. Don't forget that you were slaves ever since you can remember. You were never independent. You have new rulers now. First it was the small time rajas, whom every one accepted as the chosen ones, the Persians, Mughuls, then came the British and now the gutless immoral political Indian rulers who have nothing but their own greed in mind."

This point made me cogitate. What has changed? We have our National Anthem, which half the country doesn't want; half the country thinks that the wording of the National Anthem is outdated with so many new states being born and that it is derogatory for Indians as such and praises the British and their King; I can't argue with them. Only five states are mentioned because it was easy for the English band to play it.

What we do not know is that a Yatinder Nath Tagore wrote a song to welcome King George to the Delhi Darbar in 1911. That had nothing to do with "Jana Gana Mana...". Rabindra Nath Tagore wrote a spiritual song for the Brahmo Samaj and one of the stanzas was taken for the National Anthem! He was given the Noble Prize and then the British knighted him. He was criticized by people for having accepted the award. Tagore was the first person to return his knighthood as a protest against the Jallianwala Bagh massacre!

We have our own national flag which we wave around during matches; we are not proud enough to flaunt it on our cars. We have the American or the British flag on the rear windscreen of our cars; After a rally of the independence day celebrations, Indians flags are thrown away and then trampled upon. Further, we don't flaunt stickers of Indian states or universities on our cars but we have Wyoming or the University of Idaho or some such sticker on it, a sticker which has no relevance to anyone in India. We have our own armed forces which no one wants to join and is riddled with caste and creed problems. You have to have a quota in the armed forces for backward classes, OBCs, Muslims, Jats and the Sikhs. The Sikhs feel their number in the army is too small. The baniyas never join it. The Nepalese and Gurkhas join the Indian army because that is the only respectable thing they can do in India.

Our own youngsters want to join the IT sector where they can earn more money and serving the country in any way is the remotest thought in their mind. But ask them what is wrong with the system, and they will tell you hundreds of things along with suggestions. Ask them what they plan to do for the country and they become deaf. Ask the girls what they would like to do and the prompt answer will be that they want to be able to fend for themselves and be at par with men. So, why don't they join the armed forces and figh?t Their answer will be: — we are already there. What they mean to say is that there are 1000 odd women who are serving already. Even in that small percentage, they are being court martialed due to the allegations of and complaints of sexual harassment. The army is traditionally a man's world but if women insist on joining it, they have to be prepared for these evils of the job.

The rest of the country's women are crying themselves hoarse over the emancipation of women in India. Emancipation for them means that they can wea what they like, lesser the better; walk the ramp wearing next to nothing or the weirdest clothes that have been thought out for them; And when they wear outfits, they are so suggestive that the male libido cannot handle the sexual excitement. Emancipation has no role in it. If women become the stronger sex, I am sure they too would love to have a role reversal. But I don't see that happening in the near future. Having live-in relationship (which has been condoned by the supreme court), gay women coming out of the closet; the right to refuse to produce children and (if they have children), the right to pack them off to hostels so that they are least disturbed!"

"But then look at your male population. You thought only Oscar Wilde and Alexander The Great were gay. Look at the gay population in the entertainment world. It is sickening. The ones who are sexually normal, have so many hang ups about so many things that it is no longer funny. It all boils down to a complete absence of family and social values; a 'I-don't-give-a shit attitude!'

Where have those mothers gone, who used to teach their children morality, discipline and social values, for which, if for nothing else, India was famous? Mothers were the back bone of society. People killed for them; and died for them. Songs and poems were written about them. Where have they gone? Maybe they still exist in villages and in middle class homes where they still have the famed middle class morality; and so many others, who had single minded dedication for their children and then, the children too, responded and how! Today, they sit back and ask what has the mother ever done for them? They still expect their eighty plus mothers to do things for them!

Jyotsna, is a single mother. She adopted a little girl who has grown up to be a 10 year old lady. She tells me about her Grandmother, who was staying with her father's elder brother in Mumbai. He was 56 years old then and at a very senior post. She was a frail lady of 70 plus. The two had an argument on the breakfast table and it terminated quite suddenly when she got up and gave her son a slap! How does a 56 year old react to being slapped by his mother? He took it well. Would any mother dare to do that today, so that discipline is maintained? She would probably get slapped back!

But why do so many men lose their values so early in life. Obviously they had mothers, but then did those mothers forget to teach their children things about life in general and that it is wrong to kill and loot what belonged to other people? Maybe these mothers did not know the difference between good and evil themselves? How come we have the largest force of rioters who so regularly manifest like a swarm of angry bees, out of no where, with such regularity, time after time, to kill, burn, rape and maim their fellow human beings? Don't the rapists see their own mothers in the women they rape? What did their mothers tell them? Or, is it that they stopped listening to their mothers a long time ago?

India has been burning, not shining, for quite some time now. It is due to us that it burns. It is because of politicians that it burns. Our police force is known to be so short-sighted that it can't see beyond its nose. They missed all the bombs in Ahmedabad but later produced 24 bombs in a few days in Surat. It was wonderful to see their short sightedness being converted to X-ray Vision.

The same politicians are proceeding with such single minded devotion to split the state of Jammu and Kashmir and that too without any help from Pakistan. And if these selfish people are allowed to have their way, they will not hesitate to split the country into ten small countries and we will not be able to do anything about it.

There are 20 odd politicians who are dying to become the Prime Minister of the country. And they will stop at nothing to achieve their goal. As if by becoming the Prime Minister, they will become gods. The problem with our democracies is that there are so many politicians who will give and take an arm and a leg to become Prime Minister of the nation.

This reminds me of a darvesh from Pak Pattan, who was called Ganjey Shakkar, for there was nothing sweeter than his words. He was also from the royal family of Afganistan. I talk of Sheikh Baba Farid. He writes that once there was a rich and smart man who had tied a very beautiful turban on his head. He was walking down the road when he saw a holy man sitting in dirt on the side of the road. He sat next to the holy man after respectfully bowing his head low. But at the same time, he made sure his turban did not touch the muddy ground. Sheikh Farid said, "You foolish man, are you not aware that the head that you have tied the turban to, is bound to be destroyed itself. It is just a matter of time. Why are you giving so much importance to the turban?"

I ask these politicians the same question. Why are they giving so much value to the post of the PM of our country. It is just a temporary thing, and in the end, you will still be the same rat that you were before the race had started. To be the race winners, they sell their soul to the devil. I don't know of even one Prime

Minister of any country, let alone India, who became a god after assuming the office of the prime minister. The British youth of today wonder if the most well-known Prime Minister of Britain, Mr. Winston Churchill, was a fictional character!

I have no idea what they want to achieve? Destroying the country to become Prime Minister is short sightedness. Posterity will not forgive these people. But are they bothered about what posterity thinks of them? They are just looking for the short-term gain that they can enjoy. And then there are the pettier ones who are looking for their petty gains; followed by sycophants at every level, who, like the parasitic hyenas wait for the leftovers.

"Yes"! said SaMule. "I believe human beings are divine, created in God's own image. You people are so foolish, if I may take the liberty to call you that. You were created divine but you insist that you are the offshoots of the gorilla. You still fight over the theory of Darwin, who said things and died years ago but you do not use your own intelligence to realize that you are not created from the gorilla. Can't you see? Why are there gorillas still roaming the jungles? Why didn't all the gorillas, monkeys and orangutans become human beings? There are still millions of these animals out there and I am sure they would give a lot to be able to walk like you do, talk the way you do. Having said that, and I still hold the view that you were created in the image of God, why do you want to become animals again, even if we are better than you?" and he snorted, yet again. Oh! How I wanted to smack him.

He carried on in the same vein, "The main progress that has been made is in science. There are so many things which have been invented to enhance your comfort level. You have the motorized vehicle, aircraft, air-conditioners, refrigerators, mobile phones, computers and so many things which make your life so comfortable. But you keep building arsenals, atomic and otherwise, with the sole purpose of killing each other. There isn't a single weapon designed to kill animals only. You humans have a single minded thought process and that is to kill the other humans in ever greater numbers and in a manner that sends shivers up my spine. Why is there such an overpowering desire in humans to kill each other? Kill the other guy before he kills you, seems to be the mantra. Your existence itself is such an enigma. I have often heard people citing the large difference between the haves and have nots as the reason for the social unrest. Yes. In my opinion that would be only one reason. But if you go out and see how society has changed over the years, you will see that the people who had no place to stay, no food to eat, are living better lives today than ever before; they have access to TV and movies and through them they realize that they too can have the latest things. Jeans are being worn by every one; OK, they might not wear designer jeans which have bullet holes in them and are torn and give a beggar look to the wearer, but they definitely have access to the run-of-the-mill jeans, which makes one look more respectable than before. You come across a daily wage earner or a vegetable vendor, rickshaw pullers and taxi drivers with mobiles phones.

So, they have also moved out of the have not category and have lost the right to be called that. You will have to have a new definition of the "have not". The other day, while I was buying medicines at a chemist shop, a family of laborers from the south of India came to the same shop. After deliberating about which brand of talcum powder they should buy, they decided to let the decision lie on the shoulders of the shop owner. The head of the family asked for "the best talcum powder"! It seemed that the price was the last thing he was bothered about. All he was interested in was that his wife and kids should smell nice. The difference then lies in their monthly earnings, the kind of houses they live in and their education.

Education is not the only reason. The educated lead he good life. They become doctors, engineers, or they go into computer-related fields. Quite a few go into the financial and insurance sector where they become glorified salesmen. They are not rich people. They only feign to be rich and that will be their ultimate downfall. This is a very small percentage of the haves and they are definitely not the ones who are at loggerheads with the "have nots." In every city, there are but a few industrialists who are stinkingly rich, like the Ambanis, Tatas, the Mittals, the Bajajs and the Godrejs in Mumbai. No one has a fight with them either, for they are demi gods. Like wise the movie moghuls. These categories are the modern day untouchables. Even the 'have nots' understand that. So, they are also not the ones who create this rift between you humans. There is another breed which has incomes from sources which are unknown to most. That is the class which breeds contempt from the 'haves' and 'have nots' alike. They are definitely not the educated elite. These are the uneducated politicians, the corrupt policemen, the dons and who ever else might have the wherewithal to earn dirty money. India and the rest of the world is full of such people .It is with these people who the 'have–nots' have a grudge against. Unfortunately, the educated and the business class of 'not–so– rich' people get caught up in this group by default.

When the fight will finally come out into the open and it will come, take my word for it, all categories of the 'haves' will be caught together; irrespective of who earns clean money or who earns dirty money." The problem will arise because of the visible signs of affluence. It will not matter if one has bought a flat on a loan and he is still paying for it and will keep paying for the next twenty years; it will not matter if the car that one is driving is financed. Every one will suffer. I for one wish that I am not around to see it.

I was aware of all that crap, even if it was true. I asked SaMule, "Do you know how difficult it is for children these days to get admissions in the subjects of their choice? The cut off percentage is often 95-98 per cent. On top of that, they have to fight against the so-called stigma of being non-OBC and non-SC classes. Yes, it will soon be a stigma. If they do exceedingly well, they can get into the quota, otherwise an intelligent student is relegated to a life in a subject that he has no interest in or if his parents are affluent enough, he goes abroad to study. But once he has passed the test of fire and is settled well in life, he comes into the category of the haves and unwittingly falls prey to the 'have -have not war."

What is he supposed to do? Added to all that, is the fact that the male of the human species has traditionally been the bread winner. Suddenly, the hitherto home maker decides to add to his woes by espousing the desire to educate herself, work and earn money at par with the male. The end result is that the male is still the bread winner technically, but has to fight the OBC's, the SCs and the now, females for seats in colleges, universities and then finally jobs. He then marries such a female who works, keeps her earnings to herself while the male keeps on working as the bread winner."

"Well! Thank God for small mercies. There are no class differences in the work load of the male-female species in donkeys and the female in our world are not so evolved. In any case, even if they were, what could they have done?"

"They could have made you slog for them too!" I said.

"Ah! That would have been the day! By the way, after being in existence for thousands of years, why are you still in the caste and creed business?"

"This is because it suits our politicians to divide us into as many categories as possible so that they can divide and misrule! In India, a new religion can be started by anyone. In a movie, Satyam Shivam Sunderam, Raj Kapoor, the director, shows a mile-stone on the roadside, lying useless for years, it's paint long gone. One day, some one comes to pour water on it, another then pours a little milk and the third chappy applies vermillon as if on the forehead of a deity. This was followed by a few people coming and bowing in front of it and throwing flowers on it. Suddenly the stone is now occupying the exalted status of a deity and then they build a structure around it. Now we have an instant temple. If I go to the market place dressed in saffron clothes, open my hair and my beard, with a few of my friends gathered around me, some of them pressing my feet, a woman or two massaging my hands, I can bet my life that in a couple of days, I would have a following of a few hundred people. All I would be required to do is to keep my mouth zipped. My so called followers would say that "Baaba ji is on a "maun vrath", for three months. I would have to move my head in a horizontal or a vertical direction to whichever question I was subjected to. Chances are that I would be right at least half the time. Finish! My life is made! I can be a God man for life with a pension!

There is a person in Haryana who claims to be a modern-day god. The politicians of the twin states of Haryana and Punjab have no idea how to handle this guy. They love to hate him depending upon whose side his vote is on. He has, over the years collected thousands of followers despite cases of sexual harassment, exploitation and even murder against him. The leaders of political parties have been photographed in his hallowed presence, standing with folded hands! And he himself is seated on an elevated stage! How can they initiate cases against him and bring him to justice after the favors dished out by him in the form of the votes of his followers?" I asked.

"Do you now realize how lucky and intelligent donkeys are. We don't have political parties, we don't need gods, and we don't have other donkeys impersonating any gods. We know, as you do too, that our lives will never change because of gods. We will carry on doing the same work and continue to get the same number of abuses from you humans," said SaMule

I remained quiet; I had nothing to say. He continued, "You are besotted by your gods superficially but deep down in your heart, you are envious of Him. You want to take His place and want His powers. You want to compete against him. That is why so few of you go to the temple but throng the venues of these god-men who think they are now fit enough to compete with

God or have been ordained to represent God on earth! You don't even know if He exists. All you know is that you have been told across ages that there are gods who are great if they are on your side, but terrible people to have against you. The Greeks had gods of fire, wind, water etc. In fact they had gods of all the elements of nature. You Indians too have so many gods and goddesses that it is no longer funny. If one goes into the hills, one finds a temple in every nook and corner, some of them apparently so inaccessible that one wonders how the building material was carried to those remote places, who built them and why? And who goes there anyway?"

I looked at him and wondered at the primitive humans. They had no idea what lightening was, what torrential rains were, where did the floods come from, how did forest fires start, why did everything fall apart when the earth rumbled in an earthquake. It was but natural that men asked for forgiveness from these forces of nature, thinking that it was something very wrong that he had done to annoy whoever was causing all that destruction. And they ended up calling them gods and being scared of them. In the hills, everything becomes so dark at night that any sound would startle the local residents. Moreover, there are so many houses in the hills that were taken up as residence by suspected ghosts that the hilly people would make temples to ward them away. As man underwent mental progression and began to understand the forces of nature, he stopped being scared of them. He stopped calling them gods of this and gods of that. But the superstitions remained. Indians are very superstitious.

What is most amusing for foreigners and is a feeling in India that if the janam patris don't match, the husband will die. So, the woman gets married to a dog first and then, to the man she is supposed to wed. Now, if the dog dies, nothing is lost and no one cries. Our own beauty queen had to marry thrice. First to a banyan tree, and then to another object and finally to the man who became her husband.

The hollowness of the whole idea almost makes it sound right. The protagonists of this theory say, "The two of them are alive, nah? That was the general idea. We have keep them alive. Why are you making an issue of it?" Then, there was this millionare who died on a day when he wasn't supposed to. So, the pandits kept him alive till that auspicious day and only then, did they announce his death. They had declared that 40 more people of the family would have died due to the news. The argument was won on the same plea. So, 40 people did not die nah?

"When our one and only Amitabh Bachan fell ill recently, the whole of India went on a praying spree to whichever god they had a preference for. He recovered and their faith in their gods got a fillip. When Indian sportsmen went to Beijing for the Olympics, no one had the any hope that their sportsmen would win medals. We have a precedence. No Indian wins any medals in the Olympics. Our participation is ritualistic, just to tell the world that we too exist as a nation. Hence, an Indian representation should be there. They sent a contingent of officials which was larger than that of the sportsmen. We had reporters, TV crews and ministers who outnumbered the people who mattered.

Abhinav Bindra's parents, who are Sikhs, had a prayer meeting in the Sector 8 Guruduwara in Chandigarh. Wonder of wonders, he won a Gold medal, the first by an individual from India in 108 years. That probably cemented the place of worship and God's grace in the minds of those who were concerned. But the same thing did not happen in the case of Akhil Kumar and Vijender Kumar because they lost their bouts despite the thousands who prayed for them. They settled for the bronze medals. So this leaves us neither here nor there. Are gods choosy?

"The mool mantra of the Sikhs says:

> *Ek Onkar, Karta Purakh,*
> *Nirbhau, Nirvair,*
> *Akaal Moorat,*
> *Ajooni Saibhang Gur Prasad.*

Which when translated means :
God is the only truth, the creator,
One who has no fear,
Who has no enemy,
He is beyond incarnation,
He is self existent,
He is realized through the grace of the true master.

All Sikhs believe in this and follow accordingly. Nothing great is expected from Him, for what ever He has ordained for us in this life and the next, will be given to us when the time comes, irrespective of any marathon yagyas. But we still pray to him in the faith that he is listening and will grant us our wishes as of yesterday. In the case of Dr A.S.Bindra and family, he apparently listened. Abhinav got his gold medal. His time had come. Just fifteen days before his departure, all eyes were on Rathod and no one really remembered who Abhinav Bindra was. Some wondered what he did for a living. And then, all of a sudden, he became the hero of the nation. Rathod went into the oblivion and started batting for hockey.

The question then arises: when man was primitive and in them were born people who were superior souls; they wanted to remove the primitive man from the darkness in which he existed, almost like an animal. He was only a bit more evolved. They preached the goodness of God. Since the word of mouth vanishes with time, they chose to bring whatever they preached into the written form. That is how the Jews had their Talmud, the Christians had their Bible, the Hindus had their Gita, the Muslims their Quran and the Sikhs their Sri Guru Granth Sahib. These are the sacred books that have sustained generations of mankind over the years. But these words of the enlightened ones did not affect humans equally because we had our share of saints and monsters. The monsters tried to create as much evil as they could monstrously create. Saints, saints tried their level best to negate the effects of these monsters. Obviously, the saints won because man still exists and their trust in the almighty is still there."

SaMule had a confused look on his face."If there were so many people reading the good books down the ages, should they have been killing millions of their kind? Look at the history of the world. The number of wars that have been fought all over the world is so huge that I can't help but wonder at the contents of the books that you say has helped mankind down the ages. Look at India. You have been fighting and killing ever since you can remember. You have had holy wars on one pretext or the other. You have fought wars amongst yourselves and with invaders and killed by the thousands. You have killed thousands of people over religion in organized riots which have been recurring with such regularity that I am amazed that you people are still not bored with them. Not once did I hear, "Oh! Not again!" You eat the same food two days in a row and you refuse it on the third day. But here, it is the same scenario, again and again, year after year. May be, you get bored after some time if you haven't had an opportunity to spill some Muslim, Hindu, Christian or Sikh blood. So you throw a dead cow's head in a temple and kill hundreds of Muslims, throw a dead pig in the mosque and start a riot. Kill a Muslim and start a Hindu-Muslim riot, kidnap a Hindu girl, rape her and wipe out a whole Muslim village, kill a prime minister and murder Sikhs. Ever since the crusade by King Richard, you humans can't get your minds off each other. Don't you have anything better to do? The so called terrorists organize a blood bath by exploding bombs all over the country. When bombs explode in Pakistan, India gets blamed; bombs exploding in India and Pakistan gets blamed. Bombs exploding anywhere in the world and it is the Taliban. The fact still remains that irrespective of who is involved, they still have to be reading their ancient holy books, don't they? And they still maim, kill and torture people. I am sure this is not written in them. So why do they do it? For that matter, I have never been able to understand why humans kill each other, as in murder. What for? Haven't you had enough? Has your killing helped anyone in the past that you think it will help you now? But I must hand it you people in India. You have mastered the organization of riots and taken it so high that it has almost attained an art form. You can organize a riot on almost any issue in no time; over land, language, politics, religion, caste issues, dead animals, water or over a non-existent bridge; if a film star says she belongs to the state of U.P. and prefers to speak in the national language, Hindi, the local people will go on an instant riot/ They would break up any theatre which is screening movies of any relative of that person. A small incident would be turned into a communal riot or a caste riot. It is so easy. The dead man has to belong to some religion. The first victim will be the vehicle involved in the accident. It will be ceremoniously burnt and then, any vehicles which are unfortunate enough to pass down that road and then, anything else that might attract the fancy of the crowd shall be given to fire. Mr. Mahesh Vibhute, a student of Fergusson College, my alma mater 42 years ago, sends me this extract from ex- President Mr APJ Abdul Kalam's speech — "Why is the media so negative? Why are we, in India so embarrassed to recognize our own strengths, our achievements? Look at Dr Sudershan. He had transformed a tribal village into a self sustaining, self driving unit. There are millions of such achievements, but our media is obsessed with only bad news and failures and disasters!" This excerpt was from three vision for India.

When we are not drunk on our so called achievements, I too will become very pessimistic once the euphoria wears off. Yes, one man tried and succeeded in achieving something spectacular. Does that mean that the public will have to accept the fact that the government will do nothing for us. What ever we want to achieve will be through our own efforts. So be it. Let us do it ourselves then!

Where do we begin? We have to begin with those issues which need to be dealt with immediately. They are as follow:

- We have to start with the politicians. Murderers and those people who have corruption cases against them should never be allowed to contest elections. The weeding out of such elements should be painstakingly thorough. Agencies, which should be totally incorruptible, should make certain that these elements are the furthest from our parliament and the public alike. The safest place for them is behind bars.

- The role of the opposition should be made clear to them; that they are not in the opposition benches for the sole reason to make a ruckus and to stonewall anything that the ruling party is planning and doing. After all, a ruling party is not the countries' enemy. It is doing things for the country that they think is best for it. If they stone wall any attempted progress just because they want to impress the voting masses with their rhetoric, then the country can only go backwards. If the ruling party has won, let them go ahead and take the country forward.

- Look at what happened in Bengal where Mr. Tata wanted to have his Nano factory. People who were starving, got jobs in the factory. The state would have benefited so much from them. It was built on lands which had nothing growing on them. Compensation was given to them. But the politicians have made sure that the factory does not come up. Other states are clamoring for the project, but if one has already pumped in so much money into the project and is asked to leave, I am wondering if it is going to be feasible. And where is the guarantee that politicians in the new state will let the factory function in their region? After all, It has to be constructed on some land somewhere; there will be owners, who will have to be compensated and then the politicians, in order to take credit with the vote bank will say that the compensation wasn't enough and the factory will not be built there? The Nano has already been a given a new home in the state of Gujarat.

- It is the duty of the public to elect leaders who are Indians first and family men later. I think they should be totally answerable for their actions. If they are found to be corrupt or guilty of anti national activities or they have family ahead of the country, they should be terminated as of yesterday. But again, for this, there should be a watch dog committee which is above board and answerable only to the President. They should have the power to remove any minister, MLA or MP, if they feel that he is not fit to continue. His or her popularity should have no bearing on the punishment awarded to their likes. Corruption always begins at the top. If the Commissioner of police and his immediate subordinates are clean, then there is no chance that they will let corruption permeate down to the lowest ranks of the organization. If the prime minister of the country is corrupt, then it is bound to filter down to every level of public life and who so ever comes into direct contact with the administration. Accepting money from business organizations under the garb of the collection of party funds is, in fact, the most open form of bribery. Basically, all the ills of our country begin with the election process. Thankfully, Dr. Manmohan Singh, the present Prime Minister of India, who, in addition to being a human being par excellence, has not shown any leanings towards his family and is totally incorruptible. He has ignored the barbs from the opposition and the ignoramus alike.

- Politicians are a very integral part of the system. But who said that it is mandatory for each and every politician to be a millionaire. Can't a politician be a person who can sustain himself and his family at a decent level of survival? Why must he have property and assets worth crores? And what is that money doing for the country in any case. It lies hidden in accounts here and there. They can't use that money for they have to show an external image of austerity.

- If morality is not understood by the citizens of the country, it should come under the purview of the government. The government has to crack down on movies, cable TV and obscene songs and general vulgarity. The general public has to behave according to a set code of morality. The censor board of today should be sacked and be replaced by people who understand what morality means. I don't mind if women in India go back to the days when they had to cover themselves with a 'chuni'. No one minds Jeans or the Capris, which come just till below the knees. Showing their body in movies and fashion ramps is fine for the Americans. If countries like Pakistan (and the Arab world) can enforce a morality law, why can't we, if our women have gone out of our control? In Thailand, every thing goes in closed quarters. In fact, that is their industry. But in the street, all Thai girls are properly dressed. There is a written rule that if you have to visit the royal palace to meet the queen, every one, and I mean every one, has to be decently dressed. Jeans are not allowed. See through blouses are definitely out. The code is — dress decently or don't go to the palace. End of matter. Thailand and Malaysia are so deadly against drugs that drug pedaling carries the death sentence. A recent visit by some Indian friends to Iran meant a completely new dress code the moment they land in Iran. Everybody accepts it without any problem. The moment we step foot on our motherland, clothes are shunned as if someone on the flight had poured prickly powder on them. I agree some of us look good without them but we were talking about morality.

- Korea banned cable TV for it was affecting the morality of its countrymen. Singapore banned chewing gum, spitting and littering. The fine is so heavy that even Indians do not spit in Singapore. They cannot even dream of emptying their urinary bladder on any wall, no matter how strong the urge might be. They don't even need the donkey slogans as deterrents. The punishment would probably be caning. I really don't know if they shoot at sight or not. But the fact is that Indians behave impeccably in Singapore and other gulf countries.

- I don't know how they behave in the Scandinavian and European countries where people don't care much for laws and the dress code either. The allergic reaction to clothes started from these countries. I think it is a kick reaction to the olden era, when ladies had to wear yards and yards of cloth. They must have been fed up of them and then started the present trend. I think that those countries must be fining people for wearing too many clothes!

- Isn't it obvious why we are so well mannered outside of India? We behave impeccably where the law is very strong and the punishment harsh. The policemen in some foreign countries are honest and know that if found wanting in their duties, there will be serious repercussions. I agree that corrupt people are prevalent all over the world. But the level at which they succumb is different. In our country, the thresh-hold for a person to succumb is very low. The law has to come down harshly upon the corrupt law enforcer too.

- While we are still debating the role of the law and the law enforcers, how does one teach a country of billions where we produce generations in a matter of seconds. You teach one generation and before the clock has had the time to take a breath, millions more have arrived. Out of the generation that you think have been taught the basic rules of traffic, only 10% of them probably have understood the need for these rules and out of that 10%, probably only 2% will adhere to them. So what do you do? We should make the fines so heavy that the rule breaker will think 100 times before he even thinks of breaking them again. The fines are so heavy in the UK that people are scared out of their boots. That is what should happen here. In Nigeria, where the literacy rates were not very impressive when I was there, drivers of all kinds of vehicles followed every rule to the T. Apart from the law, the death rate on the highways of that country are enough to put the fear of the devil in any person. Their problem was speed. If there is a mishap at speeds of 120 or 130 kms an hour, it is easy to predict the outcome.

- The law mooted a good concept that in India, parents are held responsible for the conduct of their wards. But no one has been charged yet. So, there is a concept only on paper. If the parents of those minor drivers held for the numerous traffic infringements were also arrested, parents would not let their wards drive their expensive cars. If the law has been mooted, the law should be put into force and parents should be arrested too. Why haven't we heard of even one father or mother put behind bars along with his or her wards?

- Apart from coming down heavily on law breakers, the process of issuing driving licenses should be made so strict that no one can later say that he did not know the rules. The examinations, both theoretical and practical, should be conducted under strict vigil. No illiterate person should be allowed to drive. This might force people to start going to schools too. In Chandigarh, this is the practice on paper. But how does one control the touts who can circumvent any rule and for a pittance get you a license? Touts can be nullified if the person issuing the license is an honest man. The trick is to have a control over the control. God knows we have sufficient funds and more than sufficient man power.

- Religion has been the biggest problem the world over. It is the same in India. In Nigeria, Muslims and Christians are roughly equal in number. Some states are predominantly Christian and some predominantly Muslim. A family of 20 people might be equally divided between the two religions. You might even see a man who was a devout Christian turn into a devout Muslim after six months and vice versa. Has anything happened to this man? He has the same body, the same eyes, the same heart. Nothing has changed in this man physically. Only his ideas and his thoughts have changed. Thus, the eruption of sudden bloody riots between them in which hundreds of people are killed, just because their thought process has radically changed overnight. A man who was a devout Christian ever since he can remember suddenly changes over to the other faith and he is ready to kill his own erstwhile fellow believers! The same thing is happening in the USA and all over

Europe. There are so many Christians who has converted to the Muslim faith. For some reason, one does not hear of Muslims converting to the Christian faith. The great Cassius Clay is an important example. He became Mohamed Ali. There were so many more like him. This switching of religious ideologies has had a very insidious progress in India. We have had conversions from Hinduism to Christianity over the years and suddenly one finds a whole region converted to Christianity which in recent times, have been violently objected to by Hindu organizations. The reason for the conversions is absolutely different. After changing faith, these people are looked after so well by the Christian clergy and the faithful. They develop an identity of their own; they are given the respect that is due to a human being; their educational needs are met, they are free to pray in the church of their choice and they are sent abroad for further studies. But most of all, they finally stand up to be counted as human beings.

- If their parent faith denied them their basics, what is the harm if they go on another fruitful path? Every one has a right to change course. If proper respect had been accorded to them, their basic needs had been fulfilled, they would have stayed where they were, but they were not, so they remain.... degraded, poor and hungry. When this man Dara burnt a missionary along with his children in their jeep, nothing much happened to him. This reminds one of the burning of Churches belonging to the Black Americans and killing of the blacks by the Ku Klux Klan, also known as the KKK. So where is the logic? If Christ belongs to the White and the Black Americans and the Church symbolizes Christianity, then how does one church differ from the other? Just because one human being belonging to the same religion has black pigment in his skin and goes to a particular church frequented by other dark pigmented people, does it make their religion and their church different from the white pigmented people and the church they pray in?

- And who gives anyone the right to launch an attack against people of any religion? But these people, like Hitler, thought they were superior Christians and the blacks were inferior or sub human Christians. Why can't we confine our beliefs to ourselves and let other people live their lives as they choose?

- India is a huge country with so many beliefs, religions and superstitions. When I was growing up, I marveled at my country and countrymen. So many people of different castes and creeds lived under one roof, happily. In those days we did not even see so many riots. My best friends were Hindus and Muslims. Since my father got transferred so many times, and it was mostly outside Punjab, I did not have even one Sikh friend. There were so few of us outside Punjab. Never did I feel like an alien, living in a different land. Khushwant Singh, the author, Milkha Singh, the ace sprinter and Olympian, Jarnail Singh, the footballer, Bishen Singh Bedi, the Captain of the Indian cricket team and so many other Sikhs who led our armed forces had made us known in the world for our capabilities as a multi religion country which is known as Secular.

- We must have respect for the other man's beliefs and ideologies as long as they don't interfere with ours. The only way to do that is to keep religion confined within your own four walls, in religious places and in your heart, instead of trying to wear it on your sleeve. One must not bring it out into the streets. How does it affect gods if a thousand people come out in the streets to show that they belong, only to disrupt lives of other people? Have we reached a point of no return where there will never be tolerance for the other man? I doubt it. I am of the opinion that the common man is fed up of this daily violence and killing in the name of religion. Majority of the human populace is so busy trying to etch out a mere existence and worrying about where the next meal is going to come from. They have no time for all this. Religious and political leaders keep harping on the theory that no religion teaches them to kill, but the killings go on and on and on. Why?

· The general public will have to take it upon themselves to segregate those who perpetuate this hatred and are a reason for the blood shed. They have to take responsibility of their communities upon themselves and bring about the harmony that was. As it turned out, the recent bomb blasts in Delhi, Ahmedabad and Bangalore was the handiwork of young boys, who killed people not for any ideology but for the lure of the money and in that lure, the excitement of the number of people killed by each became a sort of competition among themselves. If a bomb was defused, the person responsible for it was ridiculed so that he had to make sure that he could kill more in the next attempt. In all this, they forgot that this was the country which gave them an opportunity to become what they had attained socially. All of them received education in Indian colleges and professional institutions. They forgot that this was the country which had given them food, clothing and a place to live respectfully. It was up to them to do what they could constructively do for their country; Their brothers and sisters have done the country proud by their achievements.

- When a bomb explodes somewhere, it doesn't just kill people belonging to one community. It also kills people belonging to any community who are unfortunately present there at that moment.

Bombs have not changed the destiny of any nation. No one can decimate an entire populace of a country. The fat boy could not destroy Japan via Nagasaki. Yes, bombs can disrupt lives, the peace of a neighborhood, of a country, or of the world for some time. But then life goes on. Japan went on to become a super power despite Nagasaki and Hiroshima. The 9/11 bombings in the USA killed a lot of people but that did not change anything, except the sky line. After some time, people will forget what it looked like in any case. The bombings in Iraq continue; they kill hundreds of people but life still goes on. The bombing of Marriot Hotel in Pakistan was a tragedy, but precious little damage was done to the way people lived. Many lives were lost in the Mumbai carnage of 27/11; also, there was a big loss of property. But other than that, nothing much can happen. Why can't the bombers understand this? Don't they have mirrors in their homes. Can they look at themselves in the morning and be proud of what they do to other human beings? Or, are their minds so warped that they can't identify the image anymore.

In a radio program that I heard recently, the guest was apparently a poet. He was airing his opinion about India and Indians. He said that India was such a great country and Indians were worth emulating. Even if we have lost our identity and lost contact with our glorious past for we have started wearing pants and shirts, but we have not forgotten our traditions and our faith in the sanctity of religions. Once, he said, that he was talking to a person who had an inherent dislike for a particular religion. So he presented him with a holy book of the religion that he hated and asked him to read it while sitting on the toilet seat. That person refused, saying that there was no way he could do that. A religious book has to be accorded the respect that it deserves. I laughed. You can't read their holy book sitting on the toilet seat, but you can torch the religious place where the holy book is traditionally housed and you can tear it into shreds; you can kill the people who pray in that religious place and believe in what the book says. But you can't read it sitting on the toilet seat! What a pot of hypocrites we are!

- Just today, on the 25th of September of 2008, a piece of news shocked the cobwebs from my mind. It said that 250 million people in India did not have food to eat at night. Most of them were women! The two meals that they have might not be what we call a meal. They could easily be one or two chapattis with an onion, if is available, otherwise it could only be a green chilli. When that is not available, they have to stay happy with water! And we were worrying about morality, hygiene, traffic laws, social values, family values, who gets the maximum votes, who is the hero in X or Y movies, an ex-heroine who says she has preference for Hindi and Mumbai goes into a tizzy. On the other hand, a family of four persons goes to see a movie in a multiplex, eats a few snacks with cold drinks. It ends up spending about 1500 to 2000 Rupees by the end of the evening. And this money could feed a whole familyliving below poverty line for at least two weaks.!

- It is not primarily what the common man can do for these people. It is what the Government of the land must do for these people. Building hundreds of flyovers in cities, a metro for every city in India, make stadiums to host the Commonwealth games and have hopes of hosting the Olympics is all very well for countries who can boast of being able to wipe out hunger from the face of their land. The same should be for India. Once you have made sure that all villages have the basic amenities, adequate earning avenues and every Indian gets to eat three square meals a day, then India should aim to show off its' new found status of a nuclear power. Other wise, holding games, extravaganzas, flyovers, metros, multiplexes and the likes have no meaning at all. **We might as well go back to walking with the apes.**

- High sounding jargon of the financial world like the price indexes and the Gross National Product or GDP etc have no meaning for the common man. The common urban man is interested in how much should he be earning to put food on the table for his family, get his children educated, clothe them decently, be able to house them adequately and be able to help them commute. The common villagers have a different priority which is Food! Their lives are spent looking for food to feed the family. And the head of the family is not succeeding. If he has no food, he can not be thinking about clothes or his personal hygiene; or the education of his children or the fact that his children have no traffic sense; or if they are proud of the country they belong to or if they are happy when India wins a cricket match or if an Indian by the name of Abhinav Bindra has won an individual gold in the Bejing Olympics after 108 years. He is not interested in all this. The bottom line is that he and the other 250 million of them are looking for food. He finds that no one in the country is interested in helping him find it either, least of the all, the Government. Each successive Government comes with election based slogans of 'Garibi hatao, roti, kapda aur makan'. Once they are in power, they forget all about their slogans while the opposition spends its' efforts on looking to coin newer slogans for the next election, the earlier the better.

How can man be so callous? There can be no prosperity in a country where its' people are hungry. That country does not have a right to call itself civilized. You don't have to be an Einstein to understand this simple thing. People have taken to violence, terrorism, smuggling of drugs in and out of the country and crime because they have not been unable to put three square meals on the table for their families. **Once the dirty money comes in, at least they have no fear of anyone going hungry; for hunger does not differentiate between dirty and clean money.** If Governments can not understand this basic fundamental need of human existence, they have no right to be in power. Religious agendas come later, much later. In fact they should not come in at all. God is here to stay. He is not going anywhere. But hungry people can die. Once people are clothed, fed and housed, only then can any Government say that it has earned the right to go out into the world and say that we have made it.

- In my book, it is not important what our cities look like or what the urban citizen is getting or not getting. They might look like Singapore or Zurich. It has no meaning. What is important is what do the villages of the country look like? Do they look like a village in Switzerland, Austria, UK or Germany? If they do, India is a great country. And it will be the greatest country in the world. One should learn from the Government of Bhutan. They do not harp on the indexes. They have the 'happiness quotient" of the people of Bhutan" as a priority!

- I am ashamed of the wealth that the politicians amass. So what if the ministers are rich; so what if their staff is richer; so what if their friends are hugely rich. I can only calculate the figures. Maybe I can't even do that. If the 564 odd members of Parliament have crores of rupees each, I can tell you that there is enough money in the country which is not being utilized by the Government to uplift the general condition of the people. That money belongs to the country. It should be used for the people of the country. Why is no one asking these people about that money? Where did they get it from? Was it out of their salaries? Did their fathers bequeath them that money? Chances are that their fathers did not even know that so much money existed in the world.

- What does RTI mean? If nothing is going to be done to these people, why have things like the RTI. In any case, the RTI has a limited value. The multi crore scams will be unearthed but the cheap thieves will not be punished. It is rightly said that if someone kills one or two men, he is a murderer. But if he kills thousands, he goes down in history as a great man, a conquerer. If a man rapes one woman, he is called a rapist. But if he rapes scores of men and women, as our modern day rajas he is never termed a rapist.

- The armed forces fight for the country so that we can be free, fight floods, are responsible for keeping the peace after a riot because the police can never do that, help the masses in catastrophes as in earthquakes; all this while the babus in air conditioned offices decide that they should not be at par with them in term of status and salaries(because the babus are the people who make the rules). The babu is the greatest curse the British left us with, and just before they left the Indian shores, they whispered in their ears that they are gods. That is what they started to believe. And that is what they want us to believe. And that is what a lot of us started believing. And that is what we are finally left with: gods in the administration.

- There will have to be a way to bring back our social values. Without them, the basic fiber of the country that has been eroded can never be rectified. Maybe the other ills that we face are also connected to these values systems that we let slip through our fingers. The lust for money in all walks of life has led our people to a self centered existence where they look out only for themselves. Our teachers, doctors, engineers, the police force, should be in comfortable financial levels where greed is subdued and people can concentrate on doing their job as honestly as humanly possible. But such a state is almost a fantasy in the world of today. The disparity between different strata is so huge that to be accepted in society, one has to strive hard and claw your way up the ladder. Today, the chief of the Medical Council of India succeeded in inducing in me the feeling of shame to a degree that I was not aware of. He was arrested for demanding and accepting a bribe of two crore from representatives of a medical college so that they could start admitting students for a new session. How long has he been doing it? The consequences of his actions cannot be imagined.

❑

17

SaMule Has the Last Word

Since there was no input from SaMule, I asked him for some parting pearls of wisdom, for I felt that I had come to the end of my fact finding journey, though the reasons for our fall from grace are so many that it is impossible to pin point one and say "Ahaan!!! This is why!"

He took a deep breath and said "I would call this the "Great Indian fall". It has been so great a fall that to come out of this quagmire, you Indians will definitely need divine intervention. I like the way I address you as "you Indians". I too am an Indian, though an Indian donkey.

God gave man a different brain and that brain decided upon subjugating every specie that it came across, including other human beings. Most of your problems arise because of that one trait of wanting to dominate. It is alright that you dominated most of the animal world. We don't mind. But your problems arose with the domination of man by man. Your ego was born out of that domination. It gave rise to the sense of superiority, inferiority, intelligence, beauty and comparison. They then became complexes. You incorporated emotions of love and hate into all aspects of your life.

I am sorry to keep bringing in certain factors which affect the humans of the entire world. Morality and social values have been lost the world over; maybe more in other countries than India. The way I look at things, they lost it first and you people copy whatever the white skin does. The funny part is that you have a great propensity for outdoing whatever they do and many times over. Since we are only concerned about India, let us see what happened to you on your way to your fall. And as they say, the higher you go, the harder you fall. You were at your peak hundreds of years ago. And as you 'progressed', you kept loosing your way. Dependency on money power and the inherently attached materialism and subsequent corruption then became the biggest reason for your fall.

The need to dominate others forced you to dominate over millions of your own country men by making the caste system so important in your lives. How did your ancestors ever hit upon the idea of dominating the other person by telling him that he belonged to a lower caste? It is as remarkable a concept as any. And how idiotic were those people to accept the statement that they were sub humans and even passed that thought down their generations for hundreds of years!

What you lack is respect. Respect for the self and respect for others. Most of you don't even know that the complete absence of self respect is the basis of all your subsequent actions. If you have it, then all your actions will automatically reflect it. The lack of it is the basis of all the corruption, immorality, loss of social values and national pride. You would never be a part of corruption knowing fully well that there are chances that one day, you might get caught, arrested, tried, convicted and imprisoned. Self respect will not let you do it, because of the humiliation. But today, if some one gets arrested, it doesn't affect him at all. On the contrary, he gets his fifteen minutes of fame.

Sau mein se ninyanve beiman,,
Par mera Bharat desh hai mahan!

(ninety-nine out of hundred Indians are corrupt but still, my Bharat is a great country!")

This lack of self respect makes some of your country men sell your country's secrets to the enemy, the latest being a woman who has come with thousands of excuses for being a traitor, disgrace the soldiers who died protecting your interests, show fake encounters with tomato sauce and get awards. Today, a younger sibling has the audacity to say that his elder brother will have to earn his respect. In the olden days, the respect was there, just because he was the elder of the sibling. You don't respect your parents or your teacher either. Every one is so full of the 'self' that you can't see beyond your nose anymore. These are the things that have collectively caused the **"mother of all falls,"** as you people are so fond of saying.

The best thing you had going for you were the family value system where traditional values, which had been tried and tested over the years ruled the roost. People rarely revolted against them. Children who were well bred had understood these values and just passed them on their own children.

Materialism would not have affected you so easily. Since there is no self-respect, the craze for quick money makes your younger generation do things today that their elder generation would never have done. Had they respect for themselves, society and their elders, they would never revolt against the good social norms and done what they have opted for. I am referring to girls and boys walking down the ramp, taking part in raunchy videos, dressing in dirty manner drinking and smoking and doing a host of other activities which I am not going to elaborate here. Tell me something, doctor! Why does everyone want to appear to be the same, wear the same clothes and behave in an identical manner? Is there no sense of personal identity left anymore? If one wears washed jeans or torn jeans, everyone wants to wear the same. It is the same with hair style.

Materialistic norms have changed. Earlier, everyone wanted to possess a house, a TV to go with it (a radio or a transistor set in 1960), a decent mode of conveyance (a scooter was as good and decent mode as any) and some money in the bank. So, basically there was no stampede of any kind that one could see. Now, every one wants to have as many houses as he can manage to collect. If he doesn't have money, he takes loans from the bank. The costliest car in the block should be his. Home theaters are the norm. So, if you need the best, you have to have a lot of money. If you can't earn it legally, you get it by hook and usually by crook. But if you look at it from the donkey's angle, then having surplus money in the bank has no utility. If you can't use it, then your children will misuse it, develop bad habits, stop working themselves and generally become parasites on society, rich ones at that. So how many crores do you need in the bank to satisfy your greed?

Philanthropy doesn't exist in India. If you have to donate, you people go and do that in the temple, where it is never utilized by the under privileged or by those who really need it. Remember that box from the Blood Bank Society lying in the waiting room of your clinic? It asks people to save someone today by donating money for the organization. Does any one care? Has any one ever looked at it? It falls on their retinal blind spot, as you are so fond of saying. You could say that the blood bank needs blood. So why should it go around asking for money? Eh? Why can't you use philanthropy to improve your villages? Help in hiring well paid teachers, who are teachers and not drop-outs from other streams who take up teaching only when they could not get other jobs? If you have so much money, why can't you help the government in setting up cottage industries for the villagers? I say again. Your villages have to be self sufficient. Only then can you hope for a change. There has to be a change in the attitude of your younger generation. With the change in their attitude, maybe, just maybe, the attitude of the coming generations might change. The affect of bad movies will take time to wear off. But the people who make movies will have to answer for their decision to make movies which create a bad impression on impressionable minds," he looked at me somberly and carried on.

"Look at your health minister. People are dying of starvation and he is having a running feud with your home minister over the rights of gays to have free sex! Quite a few of your people have no food, shelter or clothes to cover themselves with, and these people in high places waste their time, energy and money squabbling over matters which have no value to the world at large. They say that by allowing free sex for gays, the incidence of the dreaded AIDS will go down. As if they will have sex with only those people who are already affected. Will it go up or will it go down, pray tell me? If some people are gays, let them be. Why waste time and your energy over it. The same minister wants to stop people from smoking in public places. That is a good step. But why have rules which you can't enforce? You hardly have enough men in Khaki to control terror, riots, lawlessness, naxalites, the maoists, and even your petty thieves and traffic violators. So who is going to enforce smoking rules, keeping in mind that the men in khaki, smoke more than the general public?

If the other guy has decided to die a few years younger, let him. The funny thing is that you don't want to save those who want to be saved. You want to save the ones who want to live and die by their own rules! Whither goes your logic, kind humans?

I suppose the minister thinks that production of 'saints' will go up instantly. I am of the serious opinion that we animals are superior to you humans in many ways. When our children are born, they don't need to be looked after by the mother for years and years. Our young ones start eating on their own and start speaking on their own, the moment they are born. Your infants take 9 months to be born, nine months to a year to start walking and one to two years to start talking. During this time, they can't make the parents understand what they want, so they cry like hell. Our young ones don't do that. On the contrary, the eagle pushes its' young one out of the nest perched high up in a tree, so that it can learn how to fly. The mare nudges its newborn to stand up the moment it is born. We don't need any coaching lessons for swimming. We all know how to swim, naturally. Animals never drown, unlike humans. You drown if you haven't been taught how to swim. The only time when you refuse to drown is when you are dead, as if death teaches you how to stay afloat!

I have already said that your biggest problem is your population. It has to be curbed. I have often wondered why and how you procreate so much. I suggest you pray to the Lord's brains instead of his procreative organs. Then you will become more intelligent and maybe subdue your reproductive urges. Despite the one million children and seventy five thousand women who die every year because of tuberculosis, malnutrition, AIDS, and other diseases, the balance of the living and the dead tilts heavily

Quite a few of your inventions are based on the presumption that the only good guy is a dead one. Further, another issue is that when you kill, this is based on the "more the merrier" principle. Ever since you evolved from the apes and Kane killed his brother Abel, you have been trying to catch and slit one another's throat. Bows and arrows, spears, swords, guns, tanks, fighter aircrafts, cluster bombs, intercontinental ballistic missiles, atomic and hydrogen bombs etc. All have been invented to kill your own fellow beings, not us. Where as, in animals, quite a few of us are vegetarians. So, we don't need to kill. The carnivorous among us kill only for food. We have sporadic skirmishes over territory and for the females. We never have wars. No matter what the chemicals in our brains say, we don't have a gay society. Further, we don't have rioters we don't have thieves and murderers and we don't want OBC rights. Depravity hasn't affected our brothers in the animal world as it has, in your world. We don't have conniving minds to murder and rape.

I have wondered about your fetish for laws. You have laws against murder, looting, rape, marriage, dowry, dowry deaths, suicide, accidents and anything else that you can imagine. Despite your laws, every crime listed in your law books is carried out without fear. It is because no one is scared of your laws for the law takes an eternity to act. The perpetrator of the crime can easily hope to die a natural death before his punishment is announced by the law makers. He is thus not scared to commit any crime, knowing fully well that he will not be punished. The ones who have some clout in society are not scared, knowing that if bribes don't get them freedom, then exploitation of the huge number of loop holes in the legal system will get them off the hook. If you want a law-abiding society, the punishment will have to be swift and heavy.

Finally, before anything else, you will have to take a fresh look at your faith in God. I feel that your faith in Him has become too shallow, thus you run to so many other gods to pray to. Ironically, hardly anyone really believes in the one he is praying to. Moreover, you will have to stop competing with Him. You have to understand the basics of the act of praying. We do not have any of our own gods but we do our share of praying or braying," and he did the donkey snort yet again. Then, he said, "You were not meant to work as you ended up doing. You have made yourselves the donkeys that you had turned us into. You are donkeys of your circumstances, because this process of your fall started hundreds of years ago. It was so insidious that you hardly noticed the conversion. The present lot of you just happened to be born in India at a time when things had already gone crazy. You just kept on adding to your woes. We were not meant to do what we do; never were we meant to be at the receiving end of your sticks and your abuses. You made us do what we ended up doing. So did the horse. Look at the great elephant. Because of its' power, you began to use it as a beast of heavy burden. It started making money for you in the circus, it even learned how to play football. It helped build your temples by moving heavy stones etc. Man has successfully destroyed everything that he touched. Just the opposite of the Midas Touch!

The general man on the street will have to change and stop being so foolishly self-centered. You will have to regenerate your self-respect.

Otherwise, God will probably have to do the same thing he did many years ago... give another boat to another Noah and then destroy the world, so that a new world is created, all over again, for, in the larger scenario, the whole world is so corrupted that it has lost its' "right to exist."

For some reason, SaMule did something that I have never seen him doing. He looked at me, straight in the eye. A tear rolled down his right eye and as he blinked it away, somewhat surprised at himself, he abruptly turned and walked off. I thought it better to let him be. And then I realized that those tears should have been in my eyes and in the eyes of many more Indians. They came, very slowly, without my realizing. They came for the Mother of all falls!!

Just then, SaMule stopped, turned around very slowly and said, "Each one of you will have to take responsibility for yourselves. How are you going to do that, considering the depth of the quagmire of depravity that you all have sunk into? That is something that you will have to sort out by yourselves."

With that, he left me to my solitude, to do what one does in that state… introspect some more.

Is this what we mean by divinity? Do I still want to be divine?

Wouldn't it be better to go
back and walk with the apes?

Is this the end?

Or

Will there be a new beginning?

❑

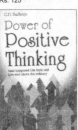

PERSONALITY DEVELOPMENT

4th Idiot
Author : B. R. Chowdhary
Rs. 150

Memory Mind& Body
Author : B. R. Chowdhary
Rs. 195

**Memorising Dictionary
Made Easy**
Author : B. R. Chowdhary
Rs. 150

Impossible... Possible...
Author : B. R. Chowdhary
Rs. 150

Memory Unlimited
Author : B. R. Chowdhary
Rs. 150

Dynamic Memory Methods
Author: B. R. Chowdhary
Rs. 150

Vocabulary @ 100 words/Hr.
Author: B. R. Chowdhary
Rs. 95

**One Minute Memory Mind
Manager**
Author : B. R. Chowdhary
Rs. 75

**Turn Your Creative Spark
Into a Flame**
Author: Joginder Singh
Rs. 95

**How To Excel When
Chips Are Down**
Author : Joginder Singh
Rs. 95

Winning Ways
Author : Joginder Singh
Rs. 150

Success Mantra
Author : Joginder Singh
Rs. 150

For A Better Tomorrow
Author: Joginder Singh
Rs. 150

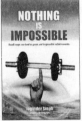

Nothing is Impossible
Author : Joginder Singh
Rs.150

Think Big Become Big
Author : Tarun Engineer
Rs. 150

**Memory Techniques
For science students**
Author : N. Roy Chowdhury
Rs. 95

DIAMOND BOOKS

X-30, Okhla Industrial Area, Phase-II, New Delhi-110020,
Phones : 41611861- 65, 40712100, Fax: 011- 41611866
E-mail : Sales@dpb.in, Website: www.dpb.in

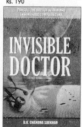

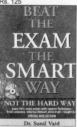